SAVING GAIA

GILBERT J. BORSA

SAVING GAIA
Copyright © 2023 by Gilbert J. Borsa

ISBN: 978-1-4866-2392-1
eBook ISBN: 978-1-4866-2393-8

Word Alive Press
119 De Baets Street Winnipeg, MB R2J 3R9
www.wordalivepress.ca

WORD ALIVE
—P R E S S—

Cataloguing in Publication information can be obtained from Library and Archives Canada.

*A book for those who think beyond themselves
and who believe in morality.*

CONTENTS

INTRODUCTION

This book does not address environmentalism directly. Rather, it discusses the behavior of our species, including family life, young men, impulse control, government, taxation, education, the economy, some decisions of the U.S. Supreme Court, our Indigenous population, religion, the health of our planet, and war.

All of the above topics are related in one way or another to the behavior of us as individuals and how we act. The cumulative effect of how eight billion human beings behave will determine whether our planet, Gaia, will live or die. That is why the book is entitled *Saving Gaia*.

I would like to thank two of my friends who helped me put this book together. Marvin Johnson has been my friend for fifty years, and he graciously listened to me advance many of my thoughts as they developed over the years. His footprints are on this book. I would also like to thank Sharon Weidman, a retired teacher, for her keen insights as she reviewed each chapter and helped me assemble the book into its current form.

ONE
MY STORY

This book is a story about how a high school dropout, a lost young white male, eventually became an accountant and mid-level manager with Revenue Canada, married a wonderful woman, and had two great children and three terrific grandchildren. Along the way, he developed several opinions about how the world came into being, and a philosophy which you could describe as religious in nature—one of hope. One which he would like to share with you.

That person is me.

My dad became deaf because of a flu in 1913 which killed more than two thousand people. My grandma was told that he would die, as he went down to eleven pounds at the age of two; she kept him alive with a teaspoon of broth every hour for two weeks. He lived, but became deaf.

Mom became deaf at the age of six while living in a poorly chinked log cabin northwest of Edmonton. The fierce northern winter winds blew through the unchinked portion of the logs and caused her to catch several diseases, which resulted in her loss of hearing. Her dad was a gold prospector and the family had moved there from Flagstaff, Arizona.

My brother, sister, and I are hearing, as our parents' deafness wasn't due to hereditary causes. For a long time, I lived in two worlds—a deaf world and a hearing world. I've always been a bit of an outsider. I understand what prejudice is like and what it's like to live in a low-income family.

I dropped out of school with a Grade Nine education and spent some time being a pool hall bum. I slowly slid downhill to the point that I became at risk of being a menial worker, or going to jail, or becoming an addict by the time I was twenty.

My friendships changed, but not for the better. I had to face up to the fact that I was ruining my life. Needing to get out of the rut I was in, I joined the Royal Canadian Navy for a period of five years at the age of seventeen.

Because I did well on an IQ test, I was trained to be a Morse code operator, designated as a Communicator Radio. I wasn't exactly the best-behaved sailor and ended up spending about a year on punishment and paid hundreds of dollars in fines when my pay was eighty dollars a month. This included being caught for swiping and pocketing my card so I could spend the night off-base. There was also the time when a friend and I grabbed two bottles of wine to party with two sisters. We slept through six alarm clocks and missed a ship under sailing orders (luckily, only a one-day trip). That would normally result in having to spend severe time in the brig.

Fortunately, we were the only two communicator radios on the base at that time, and our ship couldn't go to sea without us. Therefore, they couldn't throw us in the brig. That would really have been a black mark on my record.

This all happened in my first two years in the service.

In my third year, I was assigned to shore duty. Our training center offered B.C. Grade Eleven English and math courses. I aced the final exams with marks of 98 and 99. The Navy was experimenting with a program to give sailors the opportunity to earn a B.C. Grade Thirteen diploma and to pay their way to obtaining a university degree, with the object of becoming officers in the fleet. I was invited to join the program. I did, and that is how I got my high school diploma.

While in the program, we had to spend two hours every night on our studies and homework. I wish I had done that the following year when I enrolled in an engineering physics course. My girlfriend from Victoria had decided to come and stay with me, and the long and short of it is that I failed my year. I was given the option of returning to the fleet as a leading seaman or of resigning from the Navy. I chose to resign and return to my hometown of Winnipeg.

Because my pension contributions were returned to me, I could afford to try for a Bachelor of Science. That's when I met and married the love of my life, Donna. She helped me through the latter part of my first year in university.

Again, I didn't study properly. I was just too used to doing whatever I wanted to do, and so I failed.

I was so ashamed when I got my transcript that I left home and hitchhiked to Kenora with the intention of getting a job in the papermill. I wanted to rebuild my life there. But when I phoned Donna, she begged me to come back and assured me that we could work things out together.

I did return, and that became a turning point in my life. From that moment on, I have worked as hard as I could in every job I've had. I attended night school for seventeen years to improve my education and skills.[1] I also sought help from a psychologist to assess my vocational skills, and his advice was instrumental in turning my life around.

I got a job as a mortgage clerk for an insurance company in Winnipeg—and when the company moved to Toronto, they took me with them. I then completed a Dale Carnegie course in public speaking. There are people who think I haven't stopped talking since! I also took a three-year course in real estate appraisals.

I didn't complete my last appraisal, though, as I was offered a job back in Winnipeg as a compliance officer in Manitoba's newly formed Retail Sales Tax Branch. I spent five years there and was promoted to compliance supervisor. During this time, I completed a five-year course to become a Registered Industrial Accountant (since changed to CMA, Certified Management Accountant.)

---

[1] It may sound here like I'm taking credit for the effort of attending night school for seventeen years, but think about it—for seventeen years, my wife Donna accommodated and encouraged me all the way, despite being terribly busy herself as a teacher of the deaf, and a parent. She chauffeured our children, handled most of the household chores, and arranged our social life. She never once complained about the extra work my schooling created for her. What I did would have been impossible without her help. We were a good team.

This led to me becoming the statutory publications administrator in the Queen's Printer office for Manitoba. We were responsible for amending, printing, and distributing the loose-leaf statutes of Manitoba, selling statutory publications including the laws of the province, and distributing the *Manitoba Gazette*.

During my eight years there, we tripled our subscription base, eliminated a $25,000 annual deficit, and did it with the same group of five people, including myself.

I tried to get my best worker a raise, but the civil service decided that I was being overpaid as opposed to my worker being underpaid, since I only had a small staff. They intended to freeze my salary until it fell to the appropriate level.

The end result was that my worker returned to his home in the Netherlands, and I got a job as an income tax auditor. They replaced us with twelve people.

My bad. I should just have played the game and found room for another eight to ten staff!

During this time, I completed a four-year certificate course in public administration. I then entered an evening MBA program in government at the University of Manitoba.

As a business files income tax auditor, and then a senior business files auditor, I audited companies with sales of up to $12 million per year. To bring myself up to date on the Income Tax Act, I read it from back to front, including all its nitty-gritty details.

I was promoted to basic files auditor, where I audited companies with annual sales between $12 million and more than $1 billion. The companies I audited included those involved in manufacturing, mining, construction, agriculture, and retail sales, among others.

At the beginning of any audit, I would begin by talking to the head of the company to learn what the company was about. Many of the chief executives I spoke to were among the province's business leaders. I don't know how they felt about these conversations, but I always found them rewarding and illuminating.

For my last few years in government service, I transferred to Revenue Canada's Goods and Services Tax Branch as an audit unit manager.

During my years as an income tax auditor, I continued with my MBA studies until I reached the age of forty-two. I only completed two-thirds of the program, but between our two children needing to be chauffeured to all their activities, my wife being heavily involved with her job as a teacher of the deaf, and the demands of my job[2]—not to mention being the chairman of the Finance and Property Committee of our local United church and president of the St. James Youth Soccer Association—I ran out of steam.

I do feel guilty about quitting my MBA studies, as the university was very generous in its treatment of me. And the fact that I learned so much shows how good my professors were. I do hope they will accept my apology, should they ever have the occasion to read this book.

I was able to buy back the pension from my time in the Navy and transfer my pension from the province to the federal government, enabling me to retire at the age of fifty-six with pensionable service of thirty-four years.

In addition to my formal job experience and education, I have been an avid reader of books since I was thirteen years old. I average about two books a week, meaning that I have read about seven thousand books to date. Many of these books were works of fiction, often by writers such as Ian Fleming, Lee Child, and Dan Brown. But there is still much to be learned from fiction, since good writers conduct a great deal of research.

I continued to serve on several boards, including a church board, a senior citizens group, and as president and treasurer of our condominium corporation.

When my wife became ill, I gave up my board duties to devote my time to her. She passed from ALS on September 29, 2021, four months before her eightieth birthday, and a year and a half before our sixtieth wedding anniversary.

---

[2] I still worked as hard as I could. Which may not always have been appreciated by the taxpayers!

I like to think that I've gained some wisdom over the years, which I believe I should share before it's my time to go. That is how humanity advances. Please note that this book is written from memory, and that I have not done any serious fact-checking. Overall I do believe that I've gotten the big picture right—and as you will find out, I do mean the big picture.

I have a small bucket list. The first item was to author this book. The other two involve visiting the Hermitage Museum in St. Petersburg and the Smithsonian in Washington. I love museums and have been to some of the ones in Paris, London, Barcelona, New York, Chicago, Toronto, Ottawa, and Winnipeg, among others. I hope I will be able to visit the Smithsonian, but in view of the current state of the world I have my doubts about being able to tour the Hermitage.

TWO
CREATION

In this chapter, I will attempt to outline my limited understanding of how the universe was created, how our planet came to be, how life arose, and how humans subsequently spread across the globe. I don't speak the mathematical language of quantum mechanics, which scientists use in their discussions. But I do think it's important to have some idea of their discoveries when we get around to discussing the meaning of life and how we should conduct ourselves on this planet.

I am sure you have heard about the Big Bang. To me, it started with a huge field of potential energy developing in empty space. It built up until it was like a huge field of snow on the side of a mountain, so dense and precarious that the snap of a proverbial twig caused a huge avalanche which roared down the mountainside, destroying everything in its path, potential energy becoming reality.

I imagine that this field of energy reacted to a ripple in spacetime, and that it burst through that ripple as though being blown into a bubble-like balloon in which was contained the basis for all the mass and energy in our universe.

That is what science claims—that all the mass and energy in our entire universe was created in a single moment of time. That balloon is still expanding, with its opposite sides pulling away from each other at a rate faster than the speed of light. We will never be able to see the other side of the universe, since its light isn't fast enough to reach us.

The Big Bang happened some 13.8 billion years ago.

Science explains that the tiniest particles pop in and out of existence, and that some of these particles cling together until they reach the point at which solid particles are able to form. Both matter and antimatter are created. They destroy each other when they come into contact, but enough matter survives to create mass as we know it.

There are two kinds of quanta—one of pure energy, and another which is subjected to something called a Higgs field, possibly a Higgs boson, which causes those particles to be affected by the force of gravity. Energy is not affected by gravity, although beams of solar light can be influenced by masses as large as stars.

These slight deviations were predicted by Einstein and are used by astronomers to determine how far other suns are from the earth, and how big they are. The solid particles form into subatomic particles called quarks, which in turn form into protons, electrons, and neutrons.

Neutrons have no electric charge, protons have a positive charge, and electrons have a negative charge. Electrons are not particles according to our understanding of the word. Protons and neutrons are located deep within the atom, while electrons form a cloud-like shield around the atom.

When one atom encounters another atom, they are kept apart because of the repelling force between the negative charges surrounding each atom. In nuclear fusion, the forces involved must be strong enough to break down these negative charges.

At the Big Bang, these different particles began to form into atoms consisting of one proton, one neutron, and one electron. We know this as an atom of hydrogen. If enough hydrogen accumulates, two atoms of hydrogen are enabled to coalesce into one atom of helium, releasing an enormous burst of energy. This happens throughout the universe, and the result is that these two elements constitute ninety-eight percent of its matter.

The force of gravity causes enough hydrogen and helium to be attracted to each other to form the stars we see in the sky. The resulting release of energy causes the light we see from the stars and the heat they produce. As a star grows, the density of its core increases. Between this increase in temperature and density, electron shells disintegrate and the protons and neutrons form new elements that range from the original hydrogen all the way up the periodic chart to uranium, element 92.[3]

For example, six protons and six neutrons, when coupled with six electrons, form carbon, the basis of life on earth.

Eventually the hydrogen of a star runs out and it cools, turning red. This results in the star exploding. We see these blasts as novas, but I understand that a giant star can also become a black hole. These explosions result in the spewing of all ninety-two known elements into space. This matter then starts to accumulate around other stars, and in time becomes the basis of planets, moons, and asteroid belts.

This process of star creation, and eventual destruction, has been going on since the start of the universe and continues to this day. In five billion years, our star is expected to become a red star and eventually explode. I'm glad I won't be around when that happens!

The distance of a planet from its sun determines how much sunlight (energy) it receives, as well as its temperature. If its temperature is between zero degrees Celsius and one hundred degrees Celsius, it can support the accumulation of a certain molecule created by the merger of two atoms of hydrogen and one atom of oxygen—which is, of course, water.

Water is essential to the creation of lifeforms. Our planet was created about 4.6 billion years ago and orbits the sun in a temperate zone. As the planet got warm enough, water accumulated in pools. Surrounding elements and substances reacted in these pools, and about four billion years ago one of these substances began to replicate itself, creating the earliest lifeforms.

It wasn't until six hundred million years ago that more advanced forms of life evolved. The earliest lifeforms were precursors to all florae (plants), but some of these early lifeforms began to be able to move in search of food. They became fauna (animals). The earliest forms of trilobites

---

[3] Sanjana Curtis, "Cosmic Alchemy." *Scientific American*, January 2023, 30. Only the first twenty-six elements are initially formed. The balance are formed by atoms absorbing a neutron, and then ejecting an electron and a neutrino to form a new atom one step higher in the periodic table, or by collisions involving neutron stars.

appeared about five hundred million years ago. Animal life evolved into the age of the dinosaurs, which ruled the earth until a mass extinction event some sixty million years ago, caused by a meteor strike in the Gulf of Mexico.

Afterward mammals became the dominant form of life on land. Traces of the first biped footprints date back to eleven million years ago, but it wasn't until two hundred thousand years ago that our species of *Homo sapiens* evolved.

Twelve thousand years ago, in a period known as the Younger Dryas, either a solar flare or a comet caused an end to the last ice age. This was followed by massive flooding, which caused another mass extinction event. There are traces of that event in human prehistory, possibly including the story of Noah's Ark.

I once read that the population of early humans reached five million around the year 8,000 BCE. Humans were originally hunter-gatherers and lived in groups of about thirty[4] to one hundred and fifty members of the tribe. If the group got larger, this started to affect food gathering and created social problems. So when a tribe got too large, it split. The departing group would seek out unoccupied areas.

Tribes gathered in large groups once a year, when young males and females from different tribes formed new pairings. Our ancestors must have realized the effect of inbreeding and incest.

Humans spread throughout Africa to Europe and Asia and then expanded to North and South America. Those who travelled northward to what is now Europe reacted to the decreasing doses of ultraviolet rays. Their skin got lighter and more receptive to ultraviolet rays. This is why northern Europe was settled by white people.

Those travelling eastward were not as affected. Caucasians who live in a line stretching from India through to Spain remained quite swarthy.

Humans changed again as tribes moved into the far east. In my opinion, one's skin color is dependent on the latitude one's ancestors lived at.

---

[4] "Dunbar's Number," *Wikipedia*. Date of access: February 21, 2023 (https://en.wikipedia.org/wiki/Dunbar's_number). Dunbar's number (150) "is a suggested cognitive limit to the number of people with whom one can maintain stable social relationships."

As far as I know, there has never been a case where two persons of diverse backgrounds could not procreate because of genetic differences. I understand this is the decisive test to determine whether we are of one species. We are all siblings under the skin.

Early humans had spread to most parts of the earth by about five to seven thousand years ago, at which point there was a major hiccup. The population grew to the point that conflict arose over land use by hunter-gatherers and farmers. In addition, tribalism became a major force. Nazism, communism, and populism are current forms of tribalism which can also have serious effects.

One version of this story claims that war broke out to the extent that only five percent of men survived.[5] Apparently 9.5 million men died in what must have been the most savage wars in history, occurring over a two-thousand-year span. They ended up killing each other until there was only one man for every seventeen women.

An alternative theory suggests that there was a plague that only affected men. This is based on a DNA analysis of bones from that era. This plague would have affected the variety of the human genome for the Y portion of the human XY chromosomes.[6] The crucial point is that the gene pool of *Homo sapiens*, which we all belong to, is the source for our population of eight billion people today.

Between twelve to seven thousand years ago, humans had proliferated to the point that agrarian practices became predominant. Hunter-gatherers had increasing difficulty being able to successfully hunt game and find food. This was a major impetus in humans transitioning from hunter-gather societies to agricultural communities.

A thought I've considered is that agriculture would have needed to be practiced by women, considering the death of so many men, while the men hunted. I wonder what the social impact of this would have been!

---

[5] Jamie Seidel, "Men Nearly Caused Human Extinction 7,000 Years Ago, New Theory States," *New York Post*. May 31, 2018 (https://nypost.com/2018/05/31/men-nearly-caused-human-extinction-7000-years-ago-new-theory-states).

[6] And I thought I had enough trouble keeping up with one woman! Sorry. I just had to say it.

Agriculture eventually became the dominant occupation for humans, giving rise to the first cities.[7] Jericho in the West Bank is the oldest known city, and it developed around 9,000 BCE, followed by Byblos in Lebanon around 8,800–7,000 BCE. The bulk of the other ten oldest cities were formed between 5,000 BCE and 3,000 BCE. Interestingly, these cities were all built in the Mediterranean region.[8]

This was followed by the creation of nation-states. Several hundred years ago, humankind developed into an industrial society in many regions, followed by the current tech-based society into which we are evolving. Very soon, we will further evolve into a society where the use of robots and artificial intelligence (AI) will have dramatic effects, not to mention the changes which could be brought about by our ability to alter DNA. I hope we can do this wisely.

In playing host to all life on earth, including the plants and trees and animal forms, I think that Gaia—a.k.a. Mother Earth—became the only living organism in the known universe. Even though we are currently looking for other planets which contain life, our planet is still exceptional. Non-sentient, to be sure, but look at it this way: if Gaia dies, we all die.

Let me expound on that. You look in a mirror and see yourself intact. But when you get down to the molecular level, you would see that you're composed of millions, if not billions, of cells, each of which is a living thing. You nourish these cells with air, water, and the constituents you absorb into your bloodstream through a process we call digestion. The arteries and capillaries carry your blood to each individual cell, operating like a fast-food delivery service. Each cell has specific door openings for each of the elements it needs to repair, replicate, and energize itself. As those elements go by, the cell grabs onto what it needs. In fact, most cells in your body are replaced every seven years. In digesting food, the food is torn down to its constituent molecules by about twenty pounds of microbes in your gut. Those microbes aren't comprised of human DNA; they are foreign substances which thrive on the food you ingest. When you die, all those cells and foreign bodies die as well.

---

[7] Hermon Pontzer, "The Human Engine." *Scientific American*, January 2023, 24.
[8] "10 Oldest Cities in the World," *Oldest.org*. Date of access: February 26, 2023 (https://www.oldest.org/geography/cities).

Just like Gaia. If it dies, we die. By our actions, we can enhance Gaia to the point that it becomes a second Garden of Eden. Or we can continue to destroy it.

This entire process can be summed up in one word: evolve!

At this point, you probably think I'm trying to teach you about physics and evolution. In fact, I'm trying to present you with a different creation story than the traditional one you may have been taught.

Deep inside us, we are the same people as those who created the original stories. They faced the problem of trying to explain how the universe and we humans were created, which resulted in the story told in Genesis, among others. They also had to create guidelines as to how we should act in groups larger than thirty.[9] Their universe consisted of the sun, the moon, all the stars they could see with the naked eye, the odd messenger comet from the gods, and the ground they stood on.

There is even a creation story which postulates that the earth rode on the back of a huge turtle. Go figure! The ground the people stood on was thought to be the center of the universe.

Somewhere between 600 BCE and 400 BCE, a priest named Zoroaster, with input from Judaism, created the idea of a monotheistic god.[10] His religion, Zoroastrianism, was a major influence in the doctrines of Judaism, Christianity, Islam, and the Baha'i faith.

Around the year 1600 A.D., the telescope was invented. It raised our awareness that the universe is much larger than was thought, that the earth is round, and that it rotates around the sun instead of being the center of the universe.

Subsequently, the invention of the microscope led to a revolution in the way we perceived the human body. This resulted in the discovery of an entire world of minute lifeforms nobody had known existed until then.

This creates a problem for the world's religions. How do they respond to a different creation story? If we accept the explanation given by modern science, must we also reject what to me is the most important message in the Koran, or the Bible, or the similar work of other religions?

---

[9] There's that number again.

[10] This also provided for a destructive opposing force: Satan, like the one in Genesis.

As I said earlier, we are essentially the same people as those who lived seven thousand years ago, except we have learned so much over that period. The parts of religion which relate to how we deal with each other, what conduct is acceptable, the morals we should follow, and how we should behave are all codified in those religious books. They relate to the seven thousand years of experience that religious institutions have accumulated over that time, the rules they developed to allow us to exist in larger groups.

To me, the baby is that knowledge, while the creation story is the bathwater. I do know how important the concept of God is to religious institutions. Later in the book, I will suggest an alternative approach, but for now I'll proceed in a more conventional manner.

Before I do that, I would like to briefly discuss the measuring stick scientists use to calculate distances in the universe. It's called a lightyear, which is the speed of light multiplied by the number of seconds in a year.

The speed of light is 186,000 miles (300,000 kilometres) per second. Imagine you're in a spaceship which travels at the speed of light. Count out one second. You could have circled the earth seven times or travelled to the moon in that second. The light you see emanating from the sun took eight minutes to reach the earth.

If you multiply the speed of light by the number of seconds in the year, you will have travelled six trillion miles, or one lightyear. The distance between our earth and distant stars sometimes involves millions and billions of lightyears. It's pretty impressive to think of how big our universe is!

Space is a lot emptier than most people realize. It's largely empty, with a few hydrogen atoms floating about. There are clusters of stars and galaxies in relatively remote areas, but the universe is not densely populated. I don't know about you, but the vastness of it blows my mind. And as far as we know, the Earth is the only living thing in that universe.

I believe that most scientists do expect that other living planets will be found in time, although it's possible that earlier living planets were destroyed by societies like ours that failed to evolve sufficiently to live in harmony with their planet.

One final comment: I also expect that the scientists among us will improve and clarify the picture I have just portrayed. I am absolutely okay with that—in fact, I would encourage it. Truth is so important, especially when so many politicians seem determined to use alternate facts.

THREE

MARRIED LIFE

I consider myself one of the luckiest people on earth because I was married to a wonderful woman, my beloved Donna, for fifty-eight and a half years. I met her shortly after I got out of the Navy.

When I proposed, her mother had a fit and offered to take her to Hawaii instead. I told Donna that if we didn't get married right away, her mom would work on her until she and I were no longer a pair.

Donna arranged for our elopement, and that's what we did. After a few years, her mom and I became good friends, and at the end of her life we were in fact the best of friends.

Donna was a teacher. She started out with third graders, then taught special needs children, and eventually moved on to be a teacher of the deaf.

She spent her second year of teaching with a group of emotionally disturbed children. One day her principal received a phone call from a distraught grandmother who explained that if her grandson was not admitted to their program, the courts would send him to a juvenile detention center.

When Donna asked if she could speak to the child, the grandmother replied that she was locked in the bathroom and that her grandson was running around outside with a butcher knife.

Unbelievably, Donna agreed to meet the child. She admitted him into her program, and while there were some interesting moments that year she was the only teacher in the school who could control him.

She organized fashion shows for special needs and deaf children. When our two children were in the high school band, she oversaw two dance nights to raise money for band trips. The orchestra for those nights was a well-known professional band. They were gala affairs, which were quite successful in raising money.

She also took a hiatus of twelve years to raise our two children before returning as a teacher of the deaf.

Donna became bipolar at the age of fifty and had to go on long-term disability. It took several years to treat her manic phases, but she never had another attack once her meds kicked in. Her bipolar depression took longer to bring under control, as there were only a few medications to treat bipolar depressions in those days. I ended up searching for information on the internet and found a potential treatment which I referred to her doctor. He prescribed it. The medication worked, and then we were able to return to a more normal, less frantic life. Both Donna and I are grateful for the psychiatrist's help through the difficult times.

The worst day in both our lives happened when Donna was in a manic phase, and it's a subject I will discuss in the next chapter. I only mention it now to make it clear that once she was better, we put all this behind us. We had a good and happy life both before and after that challenging time.

When I spent my year in the Navy on shore duty, I found the time to take Arthur Murray dance lessons. That's how I learned to waltz, foxtrot, rumba, jive, and cha-cha. I did it because at the age of fifteen I had attended a country dance and discovered to my chagrin that I knew nothing about dancing. That was one of the best courses I ever took in my life, including my seventeen years of night school.

When Donna and I were courting, we had a couple of friends who could get us into the sergeant's recreation center at our local air force base. They had this jukebox which you could play all night long for free. The drinks, including cocktails, were one dollar each. We spent a lot of nights there, dancing all night long and having a wonderful time.

One night, our friend bought me six shots of his regimental drink, called Little Black Devils. It had an ounce of rum with an ounce of crème de menthe. I was okay... until I stepped outside into temperatures that were twenty degrees below zero. My blood went rushing to my head. Wham! Donna was not impressed.

We spent so many nights dancing at weddings, socials, church dances, community hall dances, and fall suppers. We even took ballroom dancing lessons later in life, which included monthly dances at which one of the groups we knew put on a demonstration of a particular dance. It was all genuine fun.

Donna had a favorite song: "Unchained Melody" by the Righteous Brothers. Whenever it came on the radio, she cranked up the music and called me to dance with her. She would hang onto me so tightly.

She passed away on September 29, 2021 from ALS. A month before, when she could hardly stand, she called me one day when that song came on. That was the last time we ever danced to that song.

If your marriage or relationship needs some jazzing up, I cannot think of a better thing than dance lessons, preferably ones where you get to hold your partner.

Donna and I knew how to play bridge, and we spent many enjoyable evenings playing with a group of eight. We also played rummoli for pennies with several other groups of eight over the years. But we didn't play poker because we found there was always someone who wanted to raise the stakes beyond our comfort level.

We had several supper clubs involving a group of eight at which the hosts provided the main course and everyone else brought a side dish like potatoes, a salad, vegetables, or a dessert. One time we had Poire's Flambe, where you ignite wine in a frying pan. We had to drop the pan to the floor in order to avoid singeing the ceiling!

If you're looking for something enjoyable to do in your life, you could do a lot worse than take cooking lessons and organize a supper club of this type. Learning to cook for two also has its advantages.

For several years, we had a crew of twelve couples who met once a month. Two couples would provide a party location, usually in one of their basements. They provided mix and nibbles, as well as music to dance to. Before the party started, there would be an activity—such as a baseball game, scavenger hunt, or skiing event. Afterward we would go to the host's place and party until the late hours. Sometimes those were late morning hours. Again, it was good, clean, inexpensive fun.

We met two of our best friends in 1972 at a United Church function. We ended up attending performances of the Winnipeg Symphony Orchestra together for fifty years, something which I continue to this very day. That's in addition to the many years we spent visiting them at their cottage, and the family events and trips we took together. Their friendship has meant so much to us over the years.

I could add many other events to the list, like our travels or family gatherings. But the main reason for writing about them isn't just to show how much we enjoyed our marriage but to give you an idea of how a couple can have a good and long-lasting relationship which includes good friends, good times, and a rich and rewarding life without having to break the bank. We didn't just sit around and drink and have boring evenings. These activities—simple card games, dancing, cooking, and so on—all involved a little bit of a challenge . Having good, clean fun makes for a better life.

We had a perfectly normal sex life. We must have made love some five thousand times over fifty-five years—that is about average, I would think. Only two of those times resulted in a pregnancy.

I once read an article indicating that in many marriages, after the age of forty, women stop having as many orgasms. I asked Donna about that. She thought for a moment and replied that she couldn't think of a single time when she hadn't had one.

Obviously she had forgotten about that one time on a Saturday morning when we were under the sheets busily having fun and our five-year-old son raced into the room, jumping on my back and whooping it up like he was riding a bucking bronco. Talk about being shocked!

We were a perfectly normal couple with a long, active, and faithful monogamous relationship. I know that if I ever had intercourse with another woman, Donna would have known, and that would have been the end of the best relationship I ever had in this life. There were a couple of times when I was sorely tempted, but this OCD brain of mine would not cooperate with my libido.

As I said, I am a normal man, and Donna was a normal woman, and together we were a good fit.

My understanding is that in India, the land of the Kama Sutra, they segregate the sex organs of men and women into three groups—small, normal, and large. They believe that sex between men and women within a group is just as enjoyable as that of any other group. You only need a compatible partner.

There is a lot more to the sexual relationship between men and women than the size of their sex organs—such as whether they like each other, their physical condition and endurance, whether they take sufficient time for foreplay, whether they are safe from pregnancy or STIs (sexually transmitted infections), etc. Choosing a good mate involves a whole lot of considerations. However, being sexually compatible with your partner can bring a lot of joy to a relationship.

You may wonder why I would include this in a book about spiritual matters. But to me, having a mutually enjoyable sex life inside a solid monogamous marriage is a significant part of having an enjoyable life and being a good person.

For Donna and myself, our primary focus was on our careers and being the parents of two special children. Raising them into successful adults who have blessed us with three exceptional grandchildren has brought much meaning, purpose, and joy into our lives. Life without them would have been so much emptier.

FOUR
TROUBLED YOUNG MALES

In this chapter, I will focus on a large group of primarily young men who find themselves in a bad place. They are discouraged under-achievers, still living at home with their parents, with little or no hope of improving their lot in life. The most desperate of them go so far as to buy an AR-15 and wreak havoc, knowing they will die in the process.

The young women of this age group are far more determined to succeed in life. For every man who goes to university, two women do. They know their sex had to fight for their place in the sun and they carry that determination with them.

So how did we get to this place?

In my grandfather's generation, married couples had families of ten to twelve children. This was suitable in an agrarian society at a time when farm machinery was still in its infancy and much farmwork was done manually.

During my father's generation, there was a massive shift from rural areas to urban cities, and the size of families dropped to three or four children. I remember that our street always had a gang of six or eight kids my age. We would play outdoors all day long except for meal breaks. If a fight broke out or someone acted up too much, a mother would pop out of her house, grab a kid by his ear, and tell him to go home. End of fight. Try that now! There was no general awareness of pedophiles. Besides, there would have been too many witnesses. We were far more independent and much less protected than the kids of today.

In the main, families have shrunk further—to one or two children. When China introduced its one child per family rule, the result was so-called princes and princesses.[11] Something similar may now be happening in many families. In a large family, you cannot be self-centered, and a close-knit family is a joy to be treasured throughout one's life. Now, however, so many people choose not to have babies that our birthrate has fallen below replacement level.[12] Families of three or four are vital to the future of our society.

If a child is overprotected and doesn't have to wrangle with his brothers as he would in a large family, and if he doesn't have to do any heavy chores around the house, is it any wonder he doesn't develop any drive?

The first thing I would tell a young man is to forget that women are women. They and every other male are his equals in this new world. He will have to compete with them on a level playing field. They will be his competitors in going on to postgraduate education, as well as in the job market.

The second thing I would tell him is that once he reaches the age of eighteen, it becomes his responsibility to learn a trade or profession that will allow him to function independently in his adult life. No one else can do that for him—it is his responsibility and his responsibility alone, no one else's. That means he must study and work hard to get ahead.

If you doubt my words, turn back to Chapter One and recall what I had to do to get out of my hellhole. Let me summarize.

Realize that your current lifestyle leads to a dead end. Determine to change yourself and create a better you in the process.

Realize that you cannot fight your way out of your situation, whether it's the ghetto or not. If you are the one in a million person who can fight like Mike Tyson, of course you can pursue a boxing career. But outside the ring, you'll be in the face of too many people if you get belligerent.

In fact, learn to smile. Your only way out of a ghetto is through education. If someone throws a punch, you have the right to defend yourself. But you can often walk away to avoid the confrontation.

---

[11] China's one-child policy has since been dropped.
[12] The average now is about 1.5 children per family compared to the ideal of 2.2 children.

I'm lucky in that I have a thick skin. I have been called so many things in this life, but I always walk away. There are times when it's okay to step up, like when someone threatens a family member or co-worker, but hopefully you can do this without resorting to violence.

Ditch the pills and watch the booze. I was lucky to grow up in an age when there were virtually no pills or narcotics available. I smoked cigarettes, heavily, from the age of thirteen to the age of thirty-two. That's when I found out how hard it is to quit an addiction. I did it because my four-year-old son begged me to quit when his sister was born. He pleaded that there was tar on all the windows and walls, and that this was threatening my family and especially my new baby girl.

So I quit on a Friday. I spent three days sick in bed. I then spent three weeks craving a drag. I spent the next three months constantly thinking about having a single drag. I went on to spend three whole years being tempted every time I went to a pub with my friends and fellow rugger players.

After three years, there came a day when the fellow next to me lit up and I almost gagged at the horrible stink.

You know how addictions develop, don't you? First you try something a little naughty, and it feels good. You try it again, and after a while it becomes a habit. That turns into a constant habit. And the next thing you know, you're hooked.[13] I'm not going to quibble about a couple of beers (unless you're an alcoholic), or even some marijuana in places where it's legal, but the hard stuff will doom you.

When we're addicted to a substance, our bodies release endorphins which elevate our mood, just as they do in sex. The difference is that sex can be good for you, while tobacco, alcohol, and opiates can destroy you.

There are places where you can get help if you can't do it on your own. Just remember my timeline: it could take you three years before you stop thinking about how sweet the hit is, even if it will kill you.

If necessary, get out of your current environment. For me, I joined the Royal Canadian Navy when I was seventeen. This turned out to be an excellent choice.

---

[13] The latest batch of drugs can become addictive the very first time you try them.

If you don't have a high school diploma, get a GED. Study hard and do your homework, no matter how difficult it is.

If you know what skill or trade you want to pursue, go for it! If not, take a battery of aptitude tests and select a career best suited to your abilities. Consult with someone who specializes in job placements, if you can afford it. Think about yourself and what you like to do, whether it's working indoors or outdoors, using a keyboard or some other tool, working alone or with people, touching or not touching other people, etc.[14] What are your hobbies—gardening, landscaping, woodworking, playing computer games? Develop your own list of likes and dislikes and take that into consideration in choosing a career.

When Donna and I retired to Gimli, a small town on the shores of Lake Winnipeg, I couldn't help but notice that the people who had the nicest houses, fanciest cars, and took the best vacations were tradespeople, especially plumbers and electricians. Those are great options, especially if you aren't academically inclined. Whatever you decide, pursue it with all your heart.

You don't have to rush the process. Remember, you have a lot of changing to do, including learning how to have a good relationship with others. Slow and steady wins the race. Having a good attitude towards your work and dealing with people will help you. Keep on smiling. People respond to a smile.

They also respond to a grim or bored face, but not in a good way.

If you follow these steps, you will reach a point where you can earn a decent living and become a solid citizen. An entire world will open to you. Will you get married and have kids? If not, what lifestyle will you pursue? It will be so much better than being dead or in jail or just eking out an existence.

People do make a lot of mistakes as teenagers. Learning from those mistakes is a big part of growing up. Facing adversity is a necessary step in becoming an adult. It develops character and self-respect. Do

---

[14] With the current aging population, there are going to be many jobs in the healthcare field. In these jobs, you will have to touch people. Would you want to be a doctor or a nurse?

not be afraid of seeking professional counselling, including the help of a psychologist. I did, and it was a big part of turning my life around.

Do work and study hard, and keep on learning when you get a job. Develop a thick skin. There are always difficult people and bosses out there. Believe in yourself. Don't get rattled or angry. Be cool. Have a good life.

If you want a good life, it's important to do things that bring you into contact with others.[15] One option is to go to church, if only for the music and lunch after the service and the chance to meet people your own age, including girls. Let closer relationships develop in their own good time.[16] Don't be too aggressive in pursuing a relationship; let a girl tell you when she is ready. If she's a decent person, the last thing she will want is to be just another one of your conquests, or to be forced into something she isn't ready for.

Good character is a key element in a good relationship. One way is to seek fun activities to do together. I like dancing or playing cards or taking in a football game—things that give you a chance to laugh and have fun. Listen as much as you speak. This is key to the art of engaging in friendly conversation.

Remember: beauty is only skin deep. There are a lot of nice girls with good brains and a good personality who are healthy, cheerful, friendly, and trustworthy. So what if they aren't a classic beauty? Are you the handsomest guy in the room?

If you're lucky, you will meet someone like my Donna.

Which brings me to the issue of sex. That is a magic wand you have in your hand. It can create enormous pleasure for you and your partner. It can also create life and spread disease! One of the cruelest things you can do is to knock a young girl up and wreck the rest of her life. It's also cruel to bring a baby into the world who will likely never know his or her father.

---

[15] Jean-Benoit Legault, "Study Suggests Our Brains Need In-Person Interaction." *Winnipeg Free Press*, January 21, 2003, F11.
[16] Daisy Yuhas, "Why Social Media Makes People Unhappy." *Scientific American*, December 2022, 72.

Having unprotected sex with someone when you know you have an STI is a crime for which some particularly bad actors have gone to jail. It's important to take precautions against pregnancy and STIs.

If you find yourself and your girlfriend getting really worked up, *stop* — and get protection. If you need to, talk to your school nurse or your doctor for advice.

Let me put it another way. If you were learning how to drive a car, you would learn how to drive safely on the right side of the road.

If you're a homosexual person, I accept your right to be true to yourself. In addition to those persons who are naturally inclined, there are many horny young men in all-boys schools, Islamic boys who aren't even allowed to look at a woman outside their family, and the millions of excess boys compared to girls in China thanks to the one child per family policy.[17]

Our sexual urges can be immensely powerful. If your means of practicing it doesn't involve criminal behavior, such as child molestation, I accept that it is the private concern of two individuals. I do have one point of irritation, though: I don't run around in bedsheets or diapers to celebrate my heterosexuality. I just find that annoying. Guess I will just have to ignore it…

Allow me to end this chapter on a serious note, with a message intended for those young men who find themselves in a deep, dark hell — those who are thinking about committing suicide or, worse yet, buying a gun to kill others knowing that they will die in the process, which is also a form of suicide.

I have spent my time in hell. When Donna came down with a bipolar disease, during one of her manic phases, she was on long-term disability from her job. She decided she would just waltz into a classroom after lunch and have a good chat with the students. It ended with her being escorted off the property. She received a letter telling her that a repeat performance could result in her being fired. There would go her income, her pension, and our economic future.

---

[17] Apparently there has been a huge increase in gay bars in China.

I was unaware of this until I came across that letter. When I found out what had happened, I realized that I couldn't control her or reason with her when she was in a manic phase.

I just lost it. I told her directly that I'd had all I could take. I stormed out the door, slamming it on my way out, and jumped into my car to go for a drive to nowhere. I was so upset that I considered suicide by truck.

I believe in the existence of the soul, and that souls pass from this life carrying the burden of having committed suicide. I couldn't do it. Eventually I calmed down and returned home, expecting to have a profoundly serious conversation with Donna.

I found out she was in hospital, having swallowed a bottle of her medications with the intent of ending her life. She had phoned our son to say goodbye, and he had immediately phoned our next-door neighbor, who ran into our house—the door was open—and found Donna already close to unconsciousness. He'd called 911 for an ambulance and they had rushed her to a hospital. Her life was saved.

That was the single worst moment of my life. The thought that my angry outburst could have caused her death scarred my soul. I am so grateful that she survived.

That's when I found out what hell was like. It has been hard for me to tell this story, as it's a private matter which I never intended to reveal. But I'm prepared to sacrifice my privacy because the story goes on to show our climb out of hell, and I need you to know that this can happen to you too.

Admit your pain. Get out of your cocoon. Do something to connect with real people, such as getting a job—any job, including a job at a fast-food outlet, or volunteer for a charity—and work hard at it. Do it with a smile. It will not be permanent.

Studies have shown that contacting others by computer or cell phone removes the benefit of human contact, and it can increase loneliness and feelings of isolation. Follow the advice in this chapter. Work and study your way to success.

Climbing out of hell was like finding ourselves at the bottom of a deep well, where we could barely make out the light at the top. There was a ladder, though, and we had to keep climbing despite feeling discouraged, tired, and in pain.

When we climbed out into the light, a miracle occurred. The doctor was finally able to prescribe the proper medications and Donna stopped having alternating episodes of mania and deep depression. We put aside everything that had happened, treated it like a bump in the road, and got on with the rest of our lives. They were good years.

As you know, Donna passed on last year, and I do miss her so.

When there is a mass shooting by a young man with an AR-15, I grieve for his soul, and for all his victims and their families. If he had the courage to commit suicide, why couldn't he have found the courage to live? It is such a tragedy on so many levels.

If you're a Christian who is in that deep dark space, and you follow the above advice, you will receive redemption for the actions which led you to that dark space. It is something you might want to discuss with your pastor, priest, or minister.

I've written about the journey I've taken to get where I am. I am satisfied that I've lived a good life, and sometime soon I will pass knowing that I like myself and that I have tried my best to be a good person. I am not famous or rich, but I couldn't care less. It is enough to know that I have given it my all. My journey is almost done.

Yours is ahead of you. I wish for you to have a successful career and a life worth living.

FIVE

EDUCATION

When I checked the internet to see whether Manitoba was implementing STEM (Science, Technology, Engineering, and Mathematics) into its education programs, I found some indications of a teacher at Balmoral Hall introducing it in her class, as well as indications of after-school programs for younger students.

I couldn't find a reference to our Department of Education considering the program. Apparently, some of our private schools are already incorporating STEM instruction. However, I am concerned that our public school students will be at a disadvantage in pursuing higher education and job opportunities in the future. I believe that STEM education better prepares students for the world of tomorrow, not only in academic areas but in trades including electricians, plumbers, and electronic technicians.

My understanding is that Canada ranks around eleventh place globally in terms of its education system. My understanding is that the United States ranked thirty-seventh out of thirty-nine countries in one survey and nineteenth in another. I've even been told that the education system in the state of Georgia is so bad that their two-year college graduates are on par with Grade Twelve students in Manitoba—and Manitoba is not at the high end of the education system in Canada.

It seems to me that a solid education helps promotes an egalitarian society. I wonder why so many American billionaires are indifferent to this problem. They are the beneficiaries of a trained workforce, so why do many of them do everything to avoid paying their fair share of tax to support the education system in their country?[18]

Our students of today will be the workers of tomorrow. We will count on them to provide the tax base to pay for our old age security. We aren't just educating kids; we're growing the adult people of the future. To get decent jobs, they'll have to develop skills and training. A solid education will give graduating high school students a good start in going on to trade school or university.

Our education system depends on having enough qualified instructors to teach specific grades and courses. In a STEM system, I would expect that a Bachelor of Science would be of assistance.

This requires foresight and planning. I think the Department of Education is aware of this need, and the need to upgrade teacher skills where required, although I have no direct knowledge about this issue.

Similarly, our education system needs to anticipate the number of tradespeople, doctors, lawyers, and all the other specialists that will be needed in four to seven years' time. It takes time to get through undergraduate and postgraduate education, so there is a considerable lag between graduation and starting someone down the path to achieve the anticipated needs of the future. I fully expect that professionals in this field are already aware of this and have plans in place to develop the workforce.

If it becomes clear that our education system will not be able to fill these needs, I recommend an extension of apprenticeship programs. I would go so far as to do so on a contractual basis, where the prospective student must demonstrate competence at a specified level—for example, people who want to go on to a medical profession and pass their MCAT would need an A or 4.0 average in the second year of a Bachelor of Science program.

I further suggest that the province offer financial assistance for the time still remaining in that student's specified degree, such as a medical degree, followed by an equal number of years for the resulting doctor to be contracted to work in the province, assigning ten to fifteen percent

---

[18] I don't have any proof in this regard; it is nevertheless my opinion.

of his income during those years to be paid back. If the doctor leaves the province before the contracted period is up, he should be required to repay any outstanding balance on advances made to him during his university years, plus a penalty of perhaps five to ten thousand dollars for a buyout—otherwise, any remaining debt should be considered to be paid in full at the end of the term.

We should think of that outstanding debt as an investment in the future of our medical profession. Something to this effect could be put in place for many different trades and professions. The number of people allowed into these programs would have to be limited to the anticipated demand. This would help eliminate massive student debt, which is a drag on the economy, and fill a future need.

I am aware that many proposals exist for retaining doctors, but it seems to me that there is a need for developing doctors. In addition, there are major hurdles to be overcome in accrediting foreign doctors who seek to immigrate to Canada. Improvements do need to be made in this area.[19]

After a student graduates and finds gainful employment, it is highly likely he will have to be retrained. This will not only affect the worker; his company will also have to adapt to a new structure. A forward-looking human resources department could be of enormous help in this process. In anticipating future workforce needs, it may be to a company's advantage to arrange for an apprenticeship program with a local trade school.

I believe programs are in place to provide support to teenage mothers, help people obtain a GED, provide training for prisoners, and rehabilitate drug users, among many other needs, but I have not made enquiries in this regard.

A major concern about the funding for our education system relates to the level to which government will meet the future need. Education must compete for money with programs that support seniors, keep up our infrastructure, adapt to climate change, as well as funding for the

---

[19] Simon Purewal, Evelyn, and Paolo Ardiles, "Canada Discourages Internationally Trained Doctors." *Winnipeg Free Press*, February 20, 2023, A7.

courts and criminal justice system, industrial base, healthcare system, and everything else the government must do.

There is only so much the government can reasonably rely on for taxation in order to raise the necessary funds. Hard choices must be made.

In my opinion, our competitiveness as a country will be rooted in how well our youth are educated. Since there is a time lag, an investment must be made upfront. Look at what happened in the United States when they began to scrimp on educating their youth, as noted above. This is aggravated by the poor start so many young American children receive in preschool programs, which lag behind most of the developed world.[20]

Our local newspapers in Manitoba have published articles about the difficulties manifesting in our school system due to a conservative government undercutting much of their funding by trying to reduce or eliminate school property taxes, replacing this income source with inadequate funding by the province out of general revenues.[21]

I think much of the above is already being actively pursued by progressive persons in industry and the education system, and I hope their thoughts far exceed what I have laid out.

During my readings, I couldn't help but take note of an article about how schoolbooks for children have started to include distorted information about climate change through the intervention of energy company representatives.[22]

---

[20] David Suskind and Lydia Denworth, "The Path to Better Childhoods." *Scientific American*, June 2022, 48.

[21] Marcela Cabezas, "Failing Grade Goes to Government, Not Schools." *Winnipeg Free Press*, January 25, 2023, A7.

[22] Katie Worth, "Climate Miseducation." *Scientific American*, July 2022, 42.

SIX

GOVERNMENT

Winston Churchill defined democracy as the worst form of government except for everything else. In one sense, he was right. There are so many factions in a democracy, all claiming that their view is the only one that should matter. There is the middle, an extreme left, and an extreme right.

The one thing that brings order to this chaos is that special "X" that a citizen gets to mark every four years or so. Every citizen, from a pauper to the richest man in the country, has the same right to vote. That vote is not only a vote for something, but also a right of recourse—a way of complaining about something the current government has done.

In American midterm elections, the "nays" are usually more likely to vote than the "ayes," as they are more motivated. The midterm election of 2022 was an exception, due to extraordinary forces, including the U.S. Supreme Court's Dodd decision, eliminating many legal protections for abortion access.

In Canada, we are fortunate in that political parties are only able to spend reasonable amounts of money during a fixed period of time before an election. This is unlike the United States, for example, where another decision by the Supreme Court, known as Citizens United, enables billionaires to pour more than a billion dollars into campaigns and attack ads designed by specialists and psychologists to influence voters. A coordinated assault on voting rights is also playing out in many American states.

Across the western world, there has been a shift towards right-wing parties in response to mass migrations of people from poorer countries. If the U.S. Democratic party doesn't come up with a policy acceptable to the population at large, they will be in trouble. Demonstrating compassion is one thing, but you can't do anything if you aren't in power.

One disadvantage in a democracy is that the long-range vision is often limited to an election cycle of roughly four years, even though so many problems require long-term solutions. But consider the alternative. In a dictatorship, there is only one answer to every problem—the one that the dictator imposes.

A benevolent dictatorship, where the dictator serves the people, such as exists in Singapore, can be highly effective in terms of long-term planning. If only so many dictators didn't change after ten or so years! Some switch seems to go off in their brains which shifts them into becoming supreme rulers instead of giving service to their country. Many become oppressive towards their population and aggressive to perceived enemies in order to justify their oppression. Their societies tend to become police states, with a stranglehold on individual freedoms, as is happening in Russia today.

Unfortunately, many autocracies in today's world are being influenced by China and Russia, and possibly India, into forming an anti-Western bloc, which may eventually influence international relations and trade.

Just imagine—a single solitary dictator in Moscow can lead the world into World War III all by himself! That's the evil of an oppressive dictatorship. Examples include Napoleon Bonaparte, Josef Stalin, Adolph Hitler, Mussolini, Saddam Hussein, and more recently Vladimir Putin. It concerns me that President Xi of China has now arranged to extend his presidency.

Communism and socialism are now in decline around the world. When East Germany stopped being a Soviet-aligned republic and joined with West Germany, the westerners initially had a lot of trouble trying to integrate East German workers into their workforce. The East German workers didn't have the same work ethic or initiative as West German workers. They were used to being plunked into a job and being told from above what to do. Under communism, production decisions were made at the top rather than being market-driven. It was an inefficient system, and subordinates kept referring issues up the ladder because they were afraid of making a mistake.

Russia became an oligarchy—a government run by a small group of people—after the collapse of the Soviet Union, and many of those oligarchs were former KGB officers who had studied western economies as part of their training.

When Putin declared war on Ukraine in 2022, some eight hundred western-based companies withdrew from Russia. I was stunned by that information, as it indicates significant change in the Russian economy, all due to Putin's rash actions.

While aristocracies are in decline, it should be noted that low inheritance taxes have created a class of millionaires and billionaires who contribute nothing to society—like the Pasha palaces in the former Ottoman empire. In that empire, it had been forbidden to kill a member of the royal family. The firstborn prince and a few brothers became members of the ruling elite, but they then faced the problem of what to do with all the other offspring. So they gave the young prince a palace and stocked it with a harem. Ultimately, the cost of these Pasha palaces bankrupted the empire.

The modern-day version of a Pasha palace is a large block of shares in a limited company which has been passed down to future generations of a person's descendants. Unless these descendants are involved in the operations of the company, their only interest is in how big their dividends will be.

In the United States, there are two major streams of thought about how the country should be governed, one based on the country's history on the coasts and the other based on people's experience in the rural areas.

In the rural areas, a settler could acquire a small tract of land, build a sod hut to get through the first winter, buy some cows, cultivate some land, and eventually grow his operation into a large ranch, becoming well-to-do in the process. He believed he did this without government help, and he thought everyone else had the same opportunity. Therefore, if a person was poor, it was his own fault.

In the coastal areas, particularly around New York, Los Angeles, and San Francisco, if an immigrant ran into a problem, he had difficulty finding a place to erect a sod hut, so those governments had to take a more supportive role. That is why New York and California are left-leaning, while many of the interior states lean to the right.

The question becomes, how do you reconcile these two different philosophies? My suggestion is to help people help themselves. If someone is willing to do the work necessary to deal with improving his station in life, he should be assisted in his quest. If he isn't willing to do the hard work, he should be provided with minimal assistance in acquiring the necessities of life.

I haven't yet emphasized the point that we are about to undergo a huge transformation in human affairs—a change as great as the transformation our civilization made while switching to an agricultural economy five thousand years ago, as well as our transformation to an industrial economy in the 1800s.

This latest transformation, which has taken place within the last fifty years, has been our collective shift to an information economy. Once they're up and running, 5G networks will transfer information some one thousand times faster than the current 4G networks.

This year, two American companies announced the initial development of a quantum computer, which has some one thousand times more operating capacity than the current largest computers in the world. The rest of the world is also working on developing this technology.

These new technologies for gathering and processing information will dwarf anything we have experienced to date, enabling governments to follow every move every citizen makes and create algorithms capable of identifying security risks. Individuals will have a greater ability than at any other time in human history to gather and use information.

It will be interesting to see how providers are affected, since almost all of this technology will involve the cloud. How will search engine capabilities and provisions be developed? We will have moved from a food economy to a things economy, and ultimately to an information-based, technological, AI, and robotic economy. Humanity will in effect have evolved into a virtually different species. How will governments handle this? We are already in the early phases of this transition.

That doesn't mean we won't any longer have a need for consumer goods or industries like transportation and construction. However, it will enormously affect how we communicate and gather information.

A major factor will be the retirement of the baby boomer generation over the next couple of decades. The workforce will shrink noticeably and the demands on the social welfare system will grow exponentially. It may become necessary for society to provide for a reduced, less demanding workweek for seniors in order to ease the burden on the economy. The salary would be coordinated with reduced retirement benefits to prevent the economy from going bankrupt. At the same time, companies will have to incorporate artificial intelligence and robotics into their systems. It will be quite a challenge!

We are approaching a time when humans will be able to connect directly to quantum computers. The biggest problem will come from having such a vast body of knowledge available to us as individuals. Algorithms will be needed to reduce this information to something that a human can comprehend.

The big question will be who has control over the design of these algorithms and whether they will direct information to select classes of people, such as the rich, and not others.

Finally, governments need to realize that if regulations become too cumbersome or picky, if they are too rigidly enforced, too difficult for the public to access easily, and subject to long bureaucratic delays, citizens and taxpayers and voters may be driven to frustration.[23] Remember the age-old KISS formula: keep it simple, stupid.

---

[23] One example comes to mind: Bill Maher and his years-long fight to be issued a simple permit to build a solar-powered sauna.

People prefer a reasonable degree of freedom. The best societies don't become overly dominating unless there is an emergency of sorts, such as a natural disaster or war.

Unfortunately, our governments face serious challenges, including the survival of our species. I hope that necessary changes can be brought about through a collaborative process that involves the public so that the public will consider itself to be part of the solution.[24]

---

[24] Ariel Procassia, "A More Perfect Algorithm." *Scientific American*, November 2022, 53. This may be of interest to those who want to create more fairly representative citizen's assemblies. This could help heal some of the rifts between the two major American parties.

SEVEN

ECONOMY

The economy of the United States and other developed countries revolves around the wages paid to laborers and other workers. Seventy percent of economic activity is consumer spending, and the major source of income that enables this activity comes from wages and earnings of workers and those in business for themselves.

Ultimately, all income arises from consumers, whose source of money is the wages paid by businesses. Businesses generate the gross earnings out of which these wages are paid. The costs of labor, or labor substitutes—cheaper foreign labor, mechanization, robots, or artificial intelligence, to name a few—are the major cost center for businesses.

Taxation diverts a portion of net business income and personal income to the government, so that the government may perform its duties and provide social services. In performing its duties, government recycles much of these taxes back to businesses and individuals, but its activities are curtailed by the amount of money it can raise through taxation.

Businesses are under intense pressure from foreign and domestic competition to reduce their direct labor costs by making the substitutions noted above. This adversely reduces the direct income of domestic laborers, and thus reduces consumer demand, affecting the entire marketplace. No business on its own is great enough to avoid this trap, which also reduces taxes which can be collected by the government.

Only the government can regulate the economy to create a level play-ing field for laborers and counteract the displacement of human beings, particularly those in the lowest-earning sixty percent of the population. Economists frown on tariffs, which if implemented, in my opinion, should only be high enough to create a level playing field on an international basis. One step would be for businesses and governments to recognize that robots and forms of artificial intelligence should be supplements to assist human labor in improving efficiency as opposed to being replace-ments for them.

Another step might be for the government to treat wages paid to laborers and other workers in a special way for income tax purposes. One way would be to simply raise the tax rate on business, but to treat the amount of tax paid through payroll deductions as a credit towards the tax payable by the company. This would help offset the loss of domestic incomes through replacement of workers.

Until recently, the United States was headed toward becoming a society where forty percent of the population lived in relative luxury and sixty percent were significantly underemployed or simply unemployed. Recent budget approvals for improving infrastructure and improving environmental projects will provide many jobs for the decades ahead.

Although there is a problem with young males now, worse would come if they and everyone else in the sixty percent started to organize. This scenario will become more likely if the education system doesn't improve.

Canada and the U.S. will face some massive infrastructure challenges over the next thirty years. These include fostering environmental and coastline protection, relocating low-lying urban centers, and bringing water to the Midwest where two major aquifers are disappearing. There will be a mass migration of people affected by clean water shortages. The disappearance of glaciers will cause a number of major rivers to dry up.

Other challenges will include coping with the massive changes to be brought about by 5G networks, phasing in robots and artificial intelligence as tools to assist people rather than replace them, meaningfully spending on defence,[25] and building a coast-to-coast, wide-gauge high-speed rail line due to the tremendous savings in energy and reduction of pollution it would enable.[26]

I would also recommend building massive desalination plants in the Gulf of Mexico and on the Pacific coast, which would pump rivers of freshwater into the Texas and California aquifers to enable sprinkler systems for watering crops and avoid turning large areas of the U.S. into deserts.

The cost of coping with these infrastructure challenges will appear to be prohibitive, but is there a way to stimulate the overall economy by carefully sequencing these projects so that the cashflow to contractors and workers can enable sufficient tax yields from a stimulated economy to offset much of the cost? That way, funds can accumulate for the next project down the line until all the projects have been completed. It would certainly provide many jobs for the sixty percent of workers who earn less, assuming enough training/retraining will be provided.

My main observation is that the economy and political system should exist for the benefit of everyone. In a free enterprise system, so much depends on the flow of capital through wages paid to the workforce, including unincorporated individual business owners. This flow of capital can be affected by the government, but we need economists to develop a model where the middle class receives enough of the flow of money to support its role as a major consumer market.

Remember the "trickle-down theory"? That has not happened. The theory has been debunked by actual results—the rich are richer; the poor are poorer.

The current model depends on population growth, but this will peak in another thirty years. It's quite a challenge! One way or another, governments will have to deal with providing for human income. Hopefully, an economic model can be developed which doesn't require a pure socialist

---

[25] The current fleets of airplanes, tanks, ships, etc. are being rendered useless through the development of hypersonic rockets by Russia and China.

[26] At this point, building high-speed rail is just a recommendation. It would reduce the massive pollution caused by air traffic.

state and which will avoid a complete collapse of society in the extreme case.[27]

No, I am not an economist. I am a retired eighty-three-year-old accountant and have been described as "an early arriver," someone who thinks about five years ahead. Speaking these thoughts is usually greeted with initial skepticism. Like when I advised our condominium board five years ago that they should install an electric car charging station as part of parkade repairs.

The suggestion to create massive desalination plants to pump lakes of water into major aquifers may seem cost-prohibitive, but what will be the cost of allowing vast areas of the Midwest and California to turn into deserts?

Similarly, improving the carrying capacity and speed of the railroad system may seem impractical, but a high-speed wide gauge system will not only create a cost-effective way to transport vast amounts of shipping—it could be a way to transport passengers and their vehicles in a comfortable setting while avoiding long drives. It would also reduce the enormous amount of air pollution attributable to air travel.

---

[27] Billionaires, beware!

EIGHT
TAXATION

I equate income tax to the condo fees I pay for my condo unit. Since I am a past president of our condo board and a former income tax auditor, the parallel is easy to see.

I own my condominium—which I had to buy and maintain. I also have to pay for my utilities and communication services. Our condo corporation is responsible for all external expenses for the property we jointly own. When the budget is prepared for the coming year, I am allocated a share of these costs based on the square footage of my unit. This is divided by twelve to determine my monthly fees. There is little leeway in making major changes to the budget—more flowers one year, for example—plus any extraordinary repair costs.

I am a citizen of Canada, as well as a resident of Manitoba and the city of Winnipeg. All three levels of government have their budgets. They assess me on my taxable income for the first two levels of government, and on my property value for the local government.

I've learned that the major portions of the budgets for all three levels of government are fixed in stone—debt payment, civil service salaries, healthcare, defence, law enforcement, etc.—and all these services have little flexibility in practice. I was once told by a former Deputy Minister of Mines in Manitoba that the leeway for significant changes in the provincial budget was less than ten percent.

When I was taking a course while at the Queen's Printer office, I wrote a report comparing the budget of a Progressive Conservative government to the budget of a New Democratic Party budget ten years later. I adjusted for minor changes in the departmental structures and used a conversion factor to update the Progressive Conservative budget so that the dollars reflected inflation over the period.

I found almost no change at all. For practical purposes, the budgets were identical. The only changes were the introduction of a Consumer Protection Bureau and Rent Control office. There was also a change in the way the law was applied in those two areas, but the actual cost difference was minor. Major cost areas, such as healthcare and education, showed virtually no change.

I appreciate the difficulty a government will experience in trying to make major changes. Either taxes must be raised or the money must come from another department. Taxpayers should pay closer attention to how campaign promises will be funded.

I once heard a proposal to introduce a flat tax system, in which a flat rate would be applied to taxable incomes over a base amount of, say, $10,000. The federal rate would be about twelve percent and the provincial rate would be roughly the same amount.

Under such a system, the CEO of a major corporation earning $2,000,000 a year would pay $477,600 in combined federal and provincial tax. His secretary, who earns $40,000, would pay $7,200 in combined tax. He is paid fifty times as much as she is, and he would pay sixty-six times as much tax—the difference being the $10,000 base. The base of $10,000 is quite low, as a person can hardly get by on an income of this amount.

A family of four would have a tax-exempt base of $40,000 and pay a tax of twenty-four percent on all combined income over and above that. There would be a benefit to a family of four, but it would hardly cover the cost of raising a family, and families are so important to our continued existence as a country.

Pension costs, pension deductions, and old age security contributions are taxable when received, so those initial payments would be a legitimate deduction from net income. A deduction for medical expenses should be allowed as well. The benefit to the government from all the work performed by charities is more than the charitable donation adjustments currently allowed, so I would continue to allow this deduction too.

I haven't pursued this proposal in depth, but I like the idea of everyone paying their fair share based on income. That way, there is no excuse for tax evasion; you just pay your fair share.

NINE

U.S. SUPREME COURT

My mom was born in the United States, so I watch a lot of U.S. news. This is my excuse for commenting on the U.S. Supreme Court, and in particular a couple of decisions it has made recently which have far-reaching effects.

My main observation is that there are two kinds of court—one which is active (such as existed during the 1960s) and one which is very conservative (such as today's court). The reason for the difference lies in the gaping hole found in the U.S. Constitution between the issues considered relevant two hundred years ago by the nation's founders and the actual country that has evolved over that time.

In the normal course of events, one would expect the Constitution to be amended to reflect changes in society. However, the mechanism for enacting changes has become so cumbersome that it is virtually impossible for Congress and the fifty state governments to pass anything, especially in view of the great divide between Democrats and Republicans.

An activist court back in the 1960s made many decisions regarding human rights, the rights of women and persons of color, the right to free speech, the loosening of laws relating to pornography and violence,[28] and school desegregation, among other things.

---

[28] In my opinion, they went too far.

The current court takes the position that if something isn't explicitly stated in the Constitution, it is a state right. That's what the reversal of the Roe vs. Wade decision is about.

The problem with this is that it creates a situation like that of slavery prior to the American Civil War, where slavery was legal in one state but not in another. It seems to me, according to my non-legal mind, that this issue concerns a fundamental right affecting half of the population, and the right of women to life, liberty, and happiness. That is a recipe for creating a mess, which is already happening.

I wonder if it would be possible for the federal government to enact a law which would allow the Supreme Court to fill the aforementioned gap with provisional rulings, subject to being overturned by the Congress, requiring perhaps a fifty or sixty percent majority. Perhaps a portion of the states (say, two-thirds) could also reverse a court decision, especially in areas which directly affect them.[29]

I believe that the issue of immigration will become one for the Supreme Court. The government should be able to figure out how many people should be allowed to enter the country, where they should go (and the right of the states to determine how many they will accept), and what to do if too many refugees end up in any one state.

On another subject, it is shocking that the Citizens United decision in 2010 has not been overturned. This decision of the Supreme Court enabled billionaires to pour up to a billion dollars into federal elections, most of which is spent on ads crafted by specialists and psychologists to influence voters. There are also deliberate campaigns to limit access to voting by disenfranchised minorities in many Republican states.

Whatever happened to the concept of one citizen, one vote, regardless of the status of the individual? Facts and reasoned arguments do not appear to matter anymore—and it is affecting the very notion that the United States is a democracy. To my untrained eye, it sure looks like an oligarchy lurking in the shadows.

---

[29] Of course, that's just a recommendation. I can hear the yelling now. It would allow the court to keep up with the evolution of society, with the assent of the federal government and a majority of the states.

The U.S. Constitution's Second Amendment was enacted in 1791. In my opinion, it was designed to enable states to create a militia at a time when most people were already armed for the purposes of hunting and self-protection, since the nearest law officer could be hours, if not days, away.

I think it is too late to change this provision in modern times, because only law-abiding citizens would willingly give up their arms, leaving the crazies capable of wreaking civil disobedience. This would leave law-abiding citizens at great risk. What an unfortunate circumstance this has become, especially at a time when there is a small but growing probability of another civil war.

The Second Amendment was enacted seventy years before the invention of the Gatling gun in 1861. I can't help but wonder if the Congress of 1791 would have enacted the same amendment if they'd known it would apply to machine guns and other weapons of war, including AR-15s—the kind of weapons used in the mass killing of schoolchildren, shoppers, and religious congregations.

The 1791 provision related to early versions of rifles, shotguns, and pistols. Accepting that these were the sorts of arms intended by Congress at the time, and excluding weapons of war, could go a long way towards reducing the severity of these mass killings.

I could go on about the U.S. electoral system, which promotes the power of fringe groups and reduces the possibility of group consensus, particularly in the nomination process, but I think I've said enough already.

TEN

INDIGENOUS POPULATION

I n the prairie regions of Canada, including my province of Manitoba, the Indigenous populations were largely hunter-gatherers who lived a semi-nomadic existence as they followed buffalo herds.

In the 1800s, settlers started to arrive, growing to millions by the early 1900s. Many of these settlers were farmers who received title to a quarter section of land. In my grandfather's case, I believe he was given something like ten dollars to help him set up his farm. One of the first things he did was to create a wall around his farm. This meant that neither Indigenous people nor buffalo could cross his property.

Between millions of farmers doing the same thing, and the buffalo hunts made famous by people like Buffalo Bill Cody, the Indigenous way of life could no longer be pursued. The Indigenous tribes got so desperate that they asked the federal government to establish reserves for the bands. Treaty One in Manitoba gave the tribes several hunting rights and control over their members, along with first options of the sale of federal land. Each person was to receive five dollars a year so he or she could afford to eat.

The first hundred years or so were brutal for Indigenous communities. In those days, the federal government placed an agent in charge of each band. These agents had enormous power over band members. Indigenous persons weren't allowed to buy liquor, and band members had to obtain permission to travel.

Early governments had to decide how to bring the Indigenous people into the nineteenth century. The tribes only spoke their own languages, and their hunting and nomadic skills were of little use in an agrarian society.

Therefore, a decision was made to create residential schools. If an Indigenous person was caught with alcohol, the band agent could take away their children and send them to one of these schools, which were run by the Catholic and Anglican churches. Children could be removed for any infraction whatsoever.

At these schools, the children were not allowed to speak their own language. They suffered many long-lasting psychological effects. It turned out that many of the children were abused, including sexual abuse, and in addition to this abuse many died.

However, one of the objectives of the program was achieved in that the children were forced to speak English or French, and because of this a notable number of them went on to become lawyers, politicians, and tradespeople.

The weakness in the residential school system, in my opinion, is that the students had no right of recourse. Remember the days when you couldn't complain about excessive force by a police officer, or a woman couldn't complain about sexual advances by her boss, or a child couldn't complain about abuses by a teacher? We now have provisions for those abuses to be reported—the right of redress.

If those Indigenous students had enjoyed the same right, much of the abuse of residential schools could have been avoided. To his credit, Pope Francis's recent visit to apologize for the Catholic Church's past behavior was a major step in the reconciliation process.

It's not that the concept of residential schools was at fault, but that the execution of it left much to be desired. I say this because my mom and dad became educated at the Manitoba Residential School for the Deaf, and their experience was positive. In addition to the regular school subjects, they used American Sign Language, while Indigenous children were forbidden to use their own languages. The attitude of teachers was entirely different for my parents, being so much friendlier and more positive.

Parents wanted their children to go to the Residential School for the Deaf, while Indigenous children were taken from their parents and forced to go to their schools.

The Manitoba Residential School for the Deaf served all four western provinces. In time, each province created their own school for deaf children, at which time the Manitoba school was discontinued as a residential school.

The graduates of this school formed many friendships which lasted a lifetime. They became good, hardworking citizens. In my dad's case, he purchased an international correspondence school course on electricity and ended up building radio sets for Mosquito bombers during WWII. This also helped him to be able to wire a house, including installing the old-fashioned fuse box that connects to the electrical grid. He ended his career operating a large cutting machine which cut steel beams, railroad ties, and other large steel components. It didn't hurt that the noise didn't bother him. I can't tell you how proud I am that he was my father.

Indigenous bands appear to be doing much better now than in those early days. Our newspapers are filled with stories about Indigenous nations doing well in pursuing their rights in court. Many Indigenous persons have gone on to become lawyers, politicians, and other professionals. They have also created many successful urban reserves. In fact, there is an urban reserve being built on the property beside my condominium under the provisions of Treaty One.

My understanding is that not all bands have shared equally in this process. One band was relocated to the northern edge of Lake Manitoba, an area which has been subjected to many floods, as the elevation there is too low. Other tribes are struggling economically.

One potentially relevant factor is that some of these tribes have hereditary chiefs, which might limit an individual's right of redress against personal abuse. I read a story a few years ago about a chief in New Brunswick who paid herself something like thirty million dollars. There have been other instances of chiefs who live luxurious lifestyles.

Some chiefs also wield enormous power over where individuals can live on a reserve. On a visit to a reserve around 1970, I noted a sharp contrast in the quality of houses just outside the reserve and those located inside the gate. The houses outside the reserve were brightly painted and in good condition. The houses within the reserve were unpainted and drab and obviously not well maintained.

I think reserves should provide for the long-term leasing of band land by band members in order to enable people to demonstrate greater pride in maintaining their homes. This could be extended to enable non-Indigenous businesses to build factories on band land and create employment opportunities for its members.

To clarify, I want Indigenous people to succeed in our society. There are enormous economic and civic safety issues at stake, as well as the people's individual wellbeing. In fact, one of the charities I donate to is called Indspire, which subsidizes university education for Indigenous youths. I'm not claiming any sort of sainthood for this, but I am putting my money where my mouth is.

ELEVEN

IMPULSE CONTROL

I t seems that every time you turn on a news broadcast, you hear of another mass shooting, murder, or other drastic action arising out of rage or panic.

I do have a suggestion on how to control fear and anger. I'd like to start by describing an everyday stressful situation—namely, a police officer pulling someone over. I'll follow that up by describing how I can control my own reactions within a matter of seconds, unless a drastic reaction is required to meet an imminent threat.

For a police officer, any slip-up during a normal stop can turn it into a high-risk procedure. The officer knows too many of his colleagues have died during these stops.

Now suppose you are a police officer. You pull a man over because of a traffic violation, or because he resembles someone who is mentioned in an APB (all-points bulletin), and it looks like the man you have pulled over is extremely agitated.

Upon closer inspection, you see that he has something in his hand— you don't know what it is, but he looks like he is going to bolt or do something crazy.

By now, you have your hand on your pistol.

Imagine that this man suddenly points at you with whatever is in his hand. You shoot him in self-defense!

Oops... it turns out to have been a cell phone.

Or imagine that he takes off like a rabbit and you shoot him.

Oops… now he's dead and you're going to have to put up with a shooting panel, and possibly a court case. Damn. Why couldn't he just have moved slowly and complied with your directions? You would have handed him his ticket, or cleared him, and he would be alive and have gotten on his way in no time at all.

It's a tragedy all the way around.

The police officer is just doing his job—and getting overexcited about it can cost a person their life! Being able to maintain your cool is worth your life.

The following is a trick I follow when I want to relax or hypnotize myself. I can give myself a command to wake at a certain hour or wake up feeling completely refreshed and in a good mood.

When I first learned this technique, I had help. If you're curious, I would suggest getting help from someone reliable who knows how to teach the method. Just remember that no one can make you do something that is against your principles while under hypnosis—I have a built-in command to immediately wake up if the hypnotist tries.

I use this procedure when it is safe to do so. There are many occasions when it isn't a good idea to relax. However, it should be safe to use this technique during a routine traffic stop. I simply take a deep breath, breathe slowly, and let the tension wash through my body, starting at the crown of my head and proceeding down to my toes as I exhale.

In a matter of seconds, I am completely relaxed.

Next I will run through the simple exercise. It shouldn't take more than ten to fifteen minutes.

Sit in a comfortable but erect chair. Relax. Take a deep breath. Concentrate on your left foot. Keep breathing slowly and deeply. Relax your foot. Shake it a little if you have to—make sure it is relaxed.

Now repeat the procedure with your right foot. Then do your left calf, your right calf, your left thigh, and your right thigh, your left hamstring, and then your right hamstring. All the while, continue to breathe deeply and slowly.

By now, your legs should be completely relaxed.

Switch to your left hand and repeat the procedure. Go on to relax your right hand, your left forearm, your right forearm, your left biceps, your right biceps, your left triceps, and then your right triceps.

Your arms should now be relaxed. Shake them a little if you feel any tension at all.

If my joints feel sore, I include them in the rotation. Keep breathing.

Next, relax your shoulders. Relax your chest, then your stomach, and then your groin. Keep breathing slowly. Relax your buttocks, the small part of your back, and the lateral muscles on your upper back.

By now, the major parts of your body below the neck should be at ease.

Relax your neck. Shake it a little to make sure the tension has gone. Then relax your scalp. It might seem strange at first. Relax your face, and then your throat. This is something you might not be used to, but imagine relaxing your esophagus and then your lungs. I feel tension leave my lungs when I do this. Then imagine relaxing your heart, followed by your stomach and inside your groin.

At this point, your whole body is relaxed.

Now stand up, take a deep breath, and exhale slowly, letting any remaining tension ooze out of your body. Your tension level should drop also.

If you are stopped by a police officer, put yourself in this relaxed state. Move slowly. If you have something in your hand, don't point it at him—hold it out and say, "Cell phone." Put on a plain face, if not an actual smile. Cooperate with the officer. If he is abusive, get his badge number and file a complaint. That is your right of recourse for unwarranted behavior.

Afterward take the ticket, or provide your ID, and explain where you're going. Hopefully you will be away in no time at all.

There is no use in getting upset. Just let him do his job. Don't take it personally. No matter what his attitude is, no one has the right to judge you. Personally, I just let someone's attitude roll off my back. I treat both positive and negative attitudes the same way—I don't let people judge me.

Being able to maintain your cool will help in many other areas, such as dealing with an angry boss or outraged customer, or when you accidentally bump into someone, or perhaps when your wife or girlfriend is angry. I don't mean for you to be a wimp. But if there are two angry people, the odds are high that something bad will happen—and you may come to regret it. If someone swings at you, of course you can defend yourself. Just don't take the first swing.

The relaxation technique I have just described is similar to the practice of meditation. It can be beneficial for human health and well-being.[30]

If you still have control issues, don't be afraid to consult with a psychologist or psychiatrist.[31]

---

[30] Matthieu Richard, Antoine Lutz, and Richard J. Davidson, "Mind of the Meditator." *Scientific American*, November 2014, 39.

[31] You may have to be referred by your family physician. I'm not sure about the current requirements.

TWELVE

WAR

History tells us that the need for living space is a driving force in war. Hitler used the concept of *lebensraum* as a justification for invading Czechoslovakia and Poland to start World War II. The Mongol hordes of Genghis Khan invaded eastern Europe because of drought in Mongolia. I earlier referred to the killing of sixteen of every seventeen men some seven thousand years ago in a desperate fight over land, which at the time was being staked by farmers from territories used by hunter-gatherers.[32]

I believe the quest for land might have been one of the motives for Vladimir Putin to invade Ukraine—for access to the sea and resources in eastern Ukraine.

In a later chapter, I will discuss the problem of displaced persons in the near future having nowhere to immigrate. This is potentially a breeding ground for violence and war.

We are presently not very aware of the wars being waged in Africa. In many developing countries, the population is continuing to grow quickly whereas the birthrate in Europe and North America is quite low.[33] It is projected that two billion extra people will be added in the next twenty to thirty years, and you can guess where much of this growth is likely to

[32] This is an assumption on my part. However, if I'm correct, it would have been the most brutal war ever fought by humans.

[33] Katie Peek, "Population Growth Is Slowing Down." *Scientific American*, March 2023, 68.

occur, adding to the problems already facing overcrowded nations.

A 2016 article postulated that the population of Africa could explode to six billion people from the 2016 level of 1.2 billion. One overall prediction is that approximately 2.4 billion people will be added in the next fifty years from our current level of eight billion people.[34]

One can see the growing tensions between India and Pakistan, two of the world's most populous countries. Also, the plains of Pakistan have recently been ravaged by severe flooding. It is also my understanding that both of these countries also have nuclear weapons.

In the case of countries around the world that are at war, whether internally or with neighbors, there will be a desire to acquire weapons of mass destruction. I wouldn't worry so much were it not for North Korea being a potential supplier of such weapons.

Most people think of nuclear war as one that takes place between superpowers where thousands of missiles are fired. I think this is incorrect and we will not see such a war unless one of the powers develops a foolproof method of negating retaliatory attacks. Even then, there are so many means of attack available that it would be difficult to mount a foolproof defense.

There are two ways in which a nuclear war could be waged.

One would be the use of conventional nuclear rockets attacking major cities and infrastructure. For example, as few as ten thermonuclear bombs could probably wipe out ten of the largest Russian cities, kill between ten to twenty million Russians, destroy perhaps eighty percent of its infrastructure, and return the country to a preindustrial stage.

Of course, the attacking country would be susceptible to severe retaliation. Although Russia has thousands of nuclear missiles in storage, they probably wouldn't have to use more than one or two hundred of these. Even so, a smaller number would still inflict a great deal of damage to the environment. Admittedly, this is just a guess.

If Russia is incapacitated as noted above, the Chinese could launch an attack in a bid to take over the eastern half of Russia, using the excuse that they must protect the Mongol descendants in that region. Russia

---

[34] Robert Engelman, "Six Billion in Africa." *Scientific American*, February 2016, 56.

would hardly be able to protect itself and would likely be reduced to the status of a failed state.

The other type of nuclear war would be to create massive EMF (electromagnetic field) explosions over a target area. This would destroy any unprotected computer chips. Trucks, cars, airplanes, communications, banking systems, and even kitchen appliances would become inoperable. In the worst-case scenario, urban areas would quickly run out of food and people would start to die within six weeks. Within three to six months, as many as eighty percent of a population could die.

To add to this joyful news, solar flares from our sun can achieve the same effect.[35] One such flare about one hundred years ago melted telegraph wires. Fortunately, the earth was in a pretechnological age at the time.

If we wanted to safeguard against this possibility, we would require all future computer chips to be protected against EMF waves. Or we could require people to keep replacement chips in a protective box for use in such an emergency.

I realize this suggestion may sound severe, but it really is a life-or-death issue. How many times do you have to use a seatbelt to protect yourself? Maybe never. Maybe once or twice.

The thought that scares me most is not World War III, but the fallout from wars in third-world countries. I wonder whether the major powers could agree to a direct intervention in any war by a third-world country which uses weapons of mass destruction. There would have to be a joint force under the auspices of the United Nations. I would recommend that the sale of any nuclear weapons by North Korea be a reason for intervention.

The current production of hypersonic weapons by the major powers may also render large flotillas obsolete. Fighter airplanes will soon be replaced by AI drones built as pilotless jets and bombers, since humans cannot take the G-forces imposed by the next generation of fighter planes. One can imagine what a battle between two drone fleets might look like.

---

[35] Johnathan O'Callaghan, "The Threat of Solar Superflares." *Scientific American*, December 2021, 60.

I just hope that the AI drones don't decide that the real enemy is us!

In my opinion, the Russian army has lost so much equipment in Ukraine, and its army has operated so poorly, that time will be required to make the necessary improvements. I think that the forces supporting the Ukrainian army should provide whatever is necessary to end this war now. Significant assistance will be required, as Russia has enormous advantages in manpower and economic strength. I would recommend an expansion of soldiers from other countries, similar to the French Foreign Legion. Also, disinformation from the Soviet-developed propaganda apparatus, directed towards its own population and those third-world countries who believe Putin's claim that the West forced his hand, needs to be counteracted. Radio Free Europe? Information warfare?

The amount of time available to respond to an attack by Russia against the United States has decreased dramatically in recent years. I don't see how the use of the nuclear football[36] by an American president could ever be justified under the present circumstances. I don't mean this facetiously, but what if the president were to be occupied in the bathroom at a critical moment? Only an AI system could operate at that speed. This increases the risk of an all-out war, but I don't see another viable option.

I cannot believe how ill-advised the war in Ukraine has been. As I write this, Putin is rushing an additional two hundred thousand troops into the battle. These troops have not been properly trained.

This reminds me of the time when the German army attacked Russia. In the first year of that war, poorly trained and equipped Russian soldiers attacked German positions en masse. For a while, it was a race to see if the Germans would run out of bullets before the Russians ran out of bodies.

If there is a massacre of the green Russian troops in Ukraine, it will only compound the senselessness of the war. What does Putin expect to win—a war-ravaged country which will likely have an underground resistance? At what cost? He will have won a country whose infrastructure

---

[36] The United States can only launch a nuclear attack with the permission of the President. An aide remains close to him at all times with a communication device, referred to as the nuclear football, which the President will use when such an order becomes necessary.

and housing he is destroying as I write this. The Ukrainians are resisting him in the same way the Afghanis resisted his predecessors! They do not want him, just as the former Soviet republics in the region do not want his dream! They know what an oppressive, top-down, poorly managed form of government is like. They didn't appreciate the USSR! Putin might, because he thrived in it, but he is the exception, not the rule.

The Americans learned the hard way in Vietnam, Cuba, Iran, and Afghanistan that if the people of a country don't want you, you should think twice about what you hope to accomplish.

It is a known fact that Russia waged an internet campaign during the last few American elections, and I suspect it was also involved in the 2022 midterms. Perhaps the U.S. is playing defense. Or is something else going on?

There is a potential for serious escalation in this area. I cannot help but wonder if former President Trump's economic troubles in the 1980s — his visits to Moscow and loans from Deutsche Bank — had anything to do with his benevolent attitude towards Russia during his time in office.

THIRTEEN

ONE WORLD OR TWO

I perceive a split between two types of government in the world, although I admit that I'm uncertain about the consequences of the split or whether the world can survive a conflict between the two systems.

One system is based on a democratic, free enterprise approach, exemplified by the governments of Europe, North America, Japan, South Korea, Australia, New Zealand, and parts of South America and Africa.

The other type is autocratic, as found in Russia, China, North Korea, and similar countries around the world, including large parts of Africa and South America.

I'm uncertain about India, although I do realize that it's supportive of Russia, dating back to when Russia supported India during the Indo-Pakistan War. Someone I play bridge with immigrated from India and is quite emphatic on this point.

This dichotomy was brought to my attention by a recent article in our local newspaper, indicating that a growing number of nations—such as India, Brazil, China, Indonesia, and many former colonial nations in Asia and Africa—are accepting Putin's assertions that NATO is responsible for the war in the Ukraine. He is portraying himself as an ally of such nations. Increased Russian trade with these nations has largely offset the effect of Western sanctions. In 2022, Russia's GDP rose by 0.3 percent.

The last paragraph of the article reads, "Today, western nations denounce Putin's aggression while tolerating, if not nurturing, at home a radical and civilizational arrogance derived from their own colonialist pasts. The world's opportunistic anti-colonialists may well win this propaganda war by default."[37]

Representatives of those post-colonial nations referred to remarks by Boris Johnson and Ron De Santis as proof of western arrogance.

Will this division between western nations and former colonial nations grow, like the division between Democrats and Republicans in the United States? The one institution which helps maintain a civil dialogue between the two factions is the United Nations. Will it be able to fulfill this role in future?

This raises another, but not totally dissimilar, question. What exactly do the words "equal" and "equality" mean? In western democracies, individuals are supposedly equal under the law. However, the reality is that the rich can afford the best lawyers to often achieve non-guilty verdicts for things others may very well go to jail for. We do not have equal opportunity, especially when you consider those born in the ghetto. Do we have equal voting rights, when many can find themselves disenfranchised by the electoral shenanigans taking place in red states?

Through my own efforts—and the help of a wonderful wife—I was able to go from being a Grade Nine dropout from a poor family to becoming a respectable (I hope) middle-class citizen. I had one asset, and that is an above-average intelligence.[38] I also had some luck along the way.

However, my achievements pale in comparison to a regular high school student by the name of Bill Gates, or any one of many millionaire athletes.

To me, the opportunity to excel is what freedom and equality mean. It's also the opportunity for someone like me to express his thoughts in a book—a gift that would most likely be denied in an oppressive society.

I understand that the more cancerous our species becomes to the continued existence of Gaia, the more likely it will be for governments to

---

[37] Pankaj Mishra, "The West Is Losing Hearts and Minds." *Winnipeg Free Press*, February 21, 2023, A7.

[38] I even have a letter from a psychologist to confirm this.

become oppressive. For our democracies to flourish, changes will have to be made to constrain the demands we place on the natural resources of our planet, and we as a species will have to adjust our inclination to become rich at all costs.

There has never been a greater need to constrain monopolies. Governments could implement measures such as those introduced by Theodore Roosevelt a hundred or so years ago when individual millionaires controlled large parts of the economy.

All of this happens at a time when China, North Korea, and Russia are pursuing a different course, seeking to obtain dominance in the weapons of war. The members of NATO will have to match these efforts. What a waste! How dangerous is this?

In the long run, these deliberations will depend on the moral code contained in our individual brains. Are you surprised? So am I! So simple! So complicated!

A new program online, called "The Atlas of Impunity," exists which can be used to rank countries on how oppressive they are towards their citizens. It ranked countries on a scale from zero (the best) to five (the worst) in five categories: unaccountable governance, abuse of human rights, conflict, economic exploitation, and environmental degradation. It then calculated a ranking of countries. The loser was Afghanistan, with a score of 4.25. The winner was Finland, with a score of 0.29.[39]

I highly recommend this resource, as it provides a clearer understanding of the degree of freedom within a country, regardless of whether that country is a democracy or an autocracy. It does seem to me that if too few people have too much money and too much power, the people suffer, whether it is a democracy or an autocracy.

The poor ranking of former colonies may be the result of inheriting a governmental system which, while highly efficient, was also designed to suppress the local population. If I could flip a switch and change the word "control" to the word "enable" in the minds of autocrats, I suspect this would reduce a potential downward spiral into war and

---

[39] "The Atlas of Impunity," *Eurasia Group*. February 17, 2023 (https://www.eurasiagroup.net/live-post/atlas-of-impunity-2023).

possible Armageddon, and leave the autocrat with a memorable place in history!

We in the West have no idea how lucky we are that our forefathers fought for our freedom, and how hard it is to establish a democracy. Witness some of the fallout from the Arab Spring.

FOURTEEN

HEALTH OF GAIA

Everyone knows that the temperature of our planet is rising and that weather events are becoming more extreme.

But the problems facing Gaia go far beyond that. Agricultural lands are facing an existential crisis. Over the next decade, vast areas of arable land will become deserts due to increasing heat and lack of water. Coastal areas will be subjected to rising ocean levels. The current prediction is a rise of two to five meters by 2050.[40]

Also, the amount of plastic in our oceans is threatening sea life—and the amount of plastic in the air is making rainwater unsafe to drink.

If our planet reaches one hundred degrees Celsius, all water on earth will evaporate and any rain that falls will be torrential in nature. Over time, the supply of freshwater will shrink. It is possible that the rainforests of Brazil will also continue to shrink, and wildfires will continue to attack our forests.

Aside from the amount of carbon dioxide we release as a species, and the amount released by forest fires, there is the possibility of nuclear war. I wonder how many damaging chemicals have already been released into the atmosphere by the war in Ukraine. Tens of thousands of explosions have already occurred, in addition to the extensive damage to buildings and infrastructure. If humankind continues down its current path, it is possible that Gaia will no longer be a habitable planet for humanity.

---

[40] Douglas Fox, "The Coming Collapse." *Scientific American*, November 2022, 33.

If there is a god, he would consider us a failed experiment. That doesn't even take into account the problems being caused by mass migrations of humans. The current rate of migration is only a drop in the bucket compared to what is to come.

Every government in the world, every industrial leader, every economist, every scientist, every doctor, and anyone with the power to make things happen has a significant role in facing the facts. They have a stake in addressing these problems.

We all have a stake. Cooperation is no longer an ideal—it is a necessity. I recently read a newspaper article which stated, "Our world needs our species to change its mind in terms of how we live on this planet—sadly, we may not be evolved enough to do so."[41]

A crucial step, to me, is to create the largest linear program ever attempted by science, to determine the maximum reasonable population of humans that can occupy this planet. This would be a population that can provide a minimum level of food, shelter, and clothing for its poorest half. A reasonable amount of arable land also needs to remain available to produce food. A certain acreage of forest is also needed to produce the oxygen that animal life requires. Similarly, there should be a minimal amount of carbon dioxide to support plant life. There also needs to be sufficient freshwater to support all life.

There must be a balance between humans, plants, land animals, sea life, nonrenewable resources, production capabilities, international transactions, freshwater, air quality, and rainfall, as these factors all interact with each other.

I realize this is a brief list of what a complete program would include.

In my opinion, we need to place a value on all known deposits of nonrenewable resources. Perhaps it would be the market value of refined ore minus the normal cost of refining it. This would be part of the above-mentioned program, so that we can determine usage rates and estimate when the resources will be depleted. Recycling programs will help, as will the possibility of extraterrestrial mining.

---

[41] Matt Henderson, "Second Thoughts." *Winnipeg Free Press*, October 29, 2022, D4.

So that is job number one—to determine the sustainable human population. Common sense tells us there must be a limit, since we humans are already having a significant impact on Gaia. The ideal population would also have to be broken down by continent—and then by nation. That's a tough one. What recourse would there be against countries who refuse to accept the broader plan?

One thing I have thought about, but haven't figured out, is the effect of people living significantly longer lives. If someone lives to the age of ninety, what are the odds of them having great-grandchildren? Will there be a stacking of generations that affects the number of people on the earth? What will be the effect of people living longer, particularly if doctors succeed in extending human life to, say, one hundred fifteen years?[42]

The age of women when they marry, and the age at which they give birth, is another factor. In many countries, the birthrate has declined below the nominal rate of 2.2 babies to achieve a stable population. This would affect the maximum desirable birthrate, the need to educate women, and potentially the need to constrain the population of individual countries.

With reference to educating women, this has an effect on the birthrate and is relevant to populations in countries which limit the rights of women. The future of our planet may be affected by the ability of Islamic women to obtain emancipation and equality in Africa. In many places, people live under dictates formulated some fifteen hundred years ago, dictates that were made in a very different environment than the one we live in now.

We also need to develop a clear picture of where environmental change will take place. Which equatorial countries will become wastelands due to extreme heat? Which coastal areas will be rendered unusable because of rising sea levels? Which areas will become uninhabitable due to desertification from lack of freshwater? Which populations will have to relocate? Where will they go?

These questions must take into consideration the fact that right-wing parties in Europe and North America are being elected largely because

---

[42] It has recently been postulated that 115 is the maximum age a human can expect to reach, based on studies conducted of the oldest people in the world.

they oppose their countries being forced to take in hordes of refugees from affected areas. This pushback will only get worse as the problem grows.

I don't expect the continent of Australia will open its floodgates to immigration. So I repeat, where will people go? Some degree of immigration will be allowed, of the best and most competent members of affected countries, but I predict that vast hordes of refugees will have no place to go, potentially creating a time bomb. I recommend that we in the western world assist third-world countries in the construction of desalination plants to prevent the widespread destruction of agrarian areas. If we can help them now, we may avert catastrophic outcomes later.

I expect that much of this information is already available. But it does need to be gathered and the missing pieces researched so significant progress can be made in planning how to cope with the coming changes. Our future depends on it.[43]

In my opinion, this information needs to be made public. I am familiar with the tendency of those in charge to hide information they think will be unpalatable to the general public, but we are all in this together. We need to know what will happen so that we can deal with it. For those in charge, the worst disasters come to them when people find out that they haven't communicated with honesty.

The current problems belong to all of us, not just a select few.

---

[43] Board of Editors, "Bringing Harmony to Earth." *Scientific American*, December 2022, 8.

FIFTEEN

RELIGION

In writing this book, I have come to realize that I keep backing into my moral code while making judgments on various issues. That realization helped me define my moral beliefs more clearly and concisely.

I believe that our earth is a living entity, just as we are living entities to the billions of individual cells in our bodies. Some people use the terms Mother Earth, or Gaia, which I prefer. The existence of these two names means that other people have had the same thought.

Gaia has an energy field which we are all part of. I do not think of Gaia as a sentient being, but I do think of it as a living body.

I know that we live in a symbiotic relationship with all other lifeforms on Gaia. And I know that I'm related to every other human being on Gaia, going back to the ancestors of our species, *Homo sapiens*, of seven to ten thousand years ago.

For several reasons, I believe that I have a soul. One is that I have a self-awareness that I find difficult to explain. Why do I feel good or bad about myself? What value system do I have? Where does my self-image come from? What exactly is this concept of me? Where do these feelings of joy, sadness, remorse, and elation come from? It can't just be because I have eyes to see or because I can smell and touch and feel.

I know that there are forces in me which are not part of my normal conscious awareness. Sigmund Freud might call this an ego. I think they come from my soul. For example, I learned how to hypnotize myself and I learned how to use chi in my body.[44]

Then there are those special times when I became hyperaware of the world, like the time I was off-duty while standing on the communications deck of the frigate I served on, in the center of a hurricane, in a light breeze, watching a struggling tugboat pull a mothballed aircraft carrier toward a scrapyard. There was a clear sky above me, the sun shining brightly through the hole as black storm clouds swirled around. As I watched our frigate writhe through waves more than thirty feet high,[45] the aircraft carrier surged upward and then smashed downward. We were there to rescue the tugboat's crew in case it started to sink.

This was one of the most amazing sights I have ever seen. My connection to Mother Earth was absolutely surreal in that moment.

I believe that my actions can be either positive or negative, and that this not only affects my soul but the energy field of Gaia as well. My actions are miniscule, but the effect of eight billion persons is not. I believe that when Gaia suffers, so do we.

As I said earlier, if Gaia dies, we die. Alternatively, if we humans become organized, we can create another Garden of Eden.

This leads me to choose to be a good person. Of course, I'm not a perfect person. I do try my best to be one, but I am also human, with all that entails.

These beliefs give me a north star by which to guide my life. I want to be able to respect and like myself and know that I've given this life my very best. I also believe that all the positive energy attached to my soul will pass to Gaia when I depart from this life. I have no idea whether it will be sentient or not.

Gosh, now I sound like Buddha. Except that he believed in reincarnation to achieve spiritual perfection and then join with the universe. Interestingly, Buddha lived at about the same time as Zoroaster, who influenced Judaism, Christianity, Islam, and Bahaism. This makes me think that everything old is new again!

---

[44] I will explain chi below.

[45] A ship is built to be flexible so that it doesn't crack in half in rough weather, like the *Titanic* did because the steel used in its construction was too hard.

I fully respect the right of people to make their own decisions about their religious beliefs.

Let me write for a moment about chi. I used to be a member of the Taoist Tai Chi Society. It doesn't teach about chi, but chi is prevalent in most Chinese martial arts. So I did my usual thing and did some reading on the subject.

The books I read explained that we can visualize the creation of a chi ball. I practiced trying to generate it inside my abdomen so that the energy would flow through my arms to my hands. The hands face each other and the energy field is felt when I bring my hands together, like two magnets repelling when you try to force similar poles to touch.

It took a while, but eventually I could form a noticeable ball, although I couldn't see it as many practitioners can.

I spoke about this with someone who had a second-degree black belt in taekwondo. She smiled and told me that she could not only create a ball, but she could see it and bounce it off a wall so that it would return to her. In fact, she had recently done so when a young student ran through the ball as it was returning to her. The child got ill and had to be sent home. She was more careful after that.

In case you're wondering, she is one of the most truthful people I know, and I completely accept her story without question.

In my most profound experience using chi, I was asked to help remove a root ball left over from building a deck and hot tub in my son-in-law's back yard. He was quoted six hundred dollars to have it removed. The contractor would have had to use two vehicles to do the job—one for a front-end loader and another to carry the root ball away.

The root ball, which was more than three feet wide and weighed over three hundred pounds, was buried in its original hole at the top of a hill overlooking the back yard. The root ball was filled with gravel, so we couldn't use a chainsaw on it. It would have to be maneuvered out of the hole, pushed about four feet to a knoll, pushed up the three-foot knoll, and then rolled down the hill without smashing it into the new hot tub.

My son-in-law asked if I could help. So, when no one was around, I got a two-by-eight board left over from building the deck and a large flat rock to see if I could get the root ball out of the hole. I was able to do so. I was then able to roll the root ball to the knoll.

I took one look at the knoll and thought I would give it one try. I got the ball halfway up, where it got stuck. I realized that if I let go of the ball, it could easily roll back down and break my leg. It had happened to a friend of mine.

What to do?

I'll try chi, I thought.

I breathed in deeply, pictured the chi running through my body, and gave the root ball a big push. Easy as pie, it rolled up and over the knoll — and I had no trouble avoiding the hot tub.

Whew! That made me a believer. At the time, I was seventy-eight years old. Not bad, eh?

My son-in-law was able to find someone to remove the root ball for two hundred dollars, so he was a happy man.

I like watching kung fu movies. When I see the actor blow somebody away using chi, I don't laugh in derision. In fact, I've tried using chi to attack a heavy punching bag in my son's basement. I forgot about Newton's third law, that there is an equal and opposite reaction, and didn't brace myself. In the process, I tore something in my shoulder which took six months to heal.

I don't like to talk about it. It's too embarrassing.

Then there was the time I used chi to perform a test that involved me squeezing a device that measured grip strength. The normal one hundred percent strength for someone in my age group was two hundred ninety pounds; I tested at three hundred ten pounds.

Coming back to my main topic, I know that human beings have latent powers known only to a few of us. I think that's part of the life energy that flows in Gaia. In my view, it is a real thing.

I believe, as noted above, that humanity can affect Gaia in positive or negative ways. I also sense a connection to the concepts of heaven and hell, both for Gaia and the individual. Gaia may not be sentient in the way we think of "God," but there are universal rules which flow from the concept of evolution.

So there you go: self-consciousness, self-hypnosis, chi, and hyperawareness all tell me that I have a spirit within me that transcends what biology tells us about being evolved apes.

When I think about the soul and what it is, I consider how the brain functions when it reacts to stimuli or makes a decision. It relies on stored information which was acquired through experience and education, including the moral guidelines of our society and decision trees embedded in our neural network. This includes all the emotional responses associated with positive and negative stimuli.

To me, the core thinking and reacting inside the brain governs our actions and emotional responses. This is the area in which our belief systems operate. I think this may be what we call the soul. Consider what happens when a person is lobotomized. He loses his emotions. In effect, he loses his soul.

I believe this area, which I now think of as the mind/soul, is always assessing everything around us, including what happens in our immediate surroundings, and pays attention to the needs of our bodily functions. I believe it also assesses us and our actions, judging whether they are "good" or "bad," depending on the moral code registered in the brain. Does it approve of us? What is our self-image? Should we be happy or sad?

I'll leave it to you to think about what your brain assesses you to be. If you don't like what you see, it's possible for you to change, and in effect redeem yourself.

It's really important to recognize the role played by the set of morals in a person's brain. Being raised a Christian in a democracy means that I have a moral code based on positive thinking and freedom. But there are those raised in different cultures which are based on dog-eat-dog values; for them, it's possible that the strong should dominate the weak and it may be okay to kill someone if they don't share the same beliefs associated with religion, economic system, etc.

There will be times when we cannot sit passively by, or we will be eaten by the bear, so to speak. It will be necessary to act in an ethical way to maintain our moral code. The actions of soldiers and police officers may result in justifiable fatalities in response to the dangers presented by others.

I recently came across two articles in an issue of *Scientific American*, a magazine which I've subscribed to going on two decades, even though I only understand half of what I read.

One article explains that the part of the brain involved in actions like assessing, reasoning, and responding is located in the ventral medial prefrontal cortex, which has two regions—one is task-oriented and the other is related to processing emotions.[46]

The other article defined a new mental disorder called a "moral injury," which is the result of attacks on a person's sense of self and their worthiness. Such afflictions are not PTSD. Rather, they arise from a person's terrible feeling that they have had to provide a service in a manner which is far below the expectations contained in their brain's moral code.[47]

A good example of a moral injury is what happened in many instances to nurses and doctors when they were overwhelmed by COVID-19. The article discussed the case of a nurse who saw a woman in immediate danger of dying but could do nothing to help her because there was no doctor or hospital bed available. It tore her apart, even though the situation wasn't her fault.

This affliction is apparently a major factor in so many doctors and nurses making the decision to leave their profession. A recent article in the *Winnipeg Free Press* highlighted this problem, noting that "such fundamentals as patient-care standards, being able to provide compassionate care and taking the time to connect with patients have become luxuries."[48]

I was struck by the relevance of the clergy, whose practitioners were able to help people suffering from moral injuries, as they had been trained in dealing with problems of this nature.

---

[46] Robert Martone, "Creating Our Sense of Self." *Scientific American*, August 2022, 86.

[47] Elizabeth Svoboda, "An Epidemic." *Scientific American*, December 2022, 52.

[48] Darlene Jackson and Linda Silas, "Nurses Want to Be Part of the Solution." *Winnipeg Free Press*, January 21, 2023, A13.

I am also aware of the energy that emanates from the human body. Consider the warmth from your partner as you hug them. That warmth you feel is energy.

Also consider that your neural network involves chemical energy. Some people claim they can see an aura of energy surrounding others. Some even claim to see different colors for these auras, indicating different types of personalities.

I have no idea if these claims are valid, but I do think that these auras are connected to the "soul." Wouldn't it be something if a scientist could measure the energy in an aura and conduct a longitudinal study to see how the aura changes over time, and whether it responds to an individual's behavior?

I cannot help but wonder if such a belief could be incorporated into the teachings of priests, ministers, and imams. I hold to the importance of religious beliefs which promote our ability to act in cooperative, constructive ways instead of dominating, destructive ways in furthering the evolution of our species.

I believe that various religions still have a significant role to play in society, given what their adherents have learned about human interactions over a period going back some seven thousand years. These religions wouldn't have existed for such a long time if they didn't fill a human need.

My personal view neither confirms nor denies the existence of God. If you think of God as the Great Architect of the universe, it makes sense that God would follow the rules of the universe he created. Any architect or builder must follow certain procedures in designing or constructing something—a building or a bridge, for example. I don't think it necessary to consider God as a Judge, however, since we shape our own soul for good or evil and any potential consequence will be self-evident as we pass on.

I think it would be beneficial for the various religions to come together and create a collective moral code to help us as individuals and as a society. Something like the Ten Commandments. Something which could apply to believers and non-believers alike.

There are those who cite all the terrible things which have happened in the name of religion, such as the Spanish Inquisition, the Crusades, the One Hundred Years War between Catholics and Protestants, the current dispute between the Shia and Sunni sects of Islam, the activities of ISIS, our recent experience with residential schools for the Indigenous, and abuse charges against members of the clergy. Many wars have to do with the need to dominate others for land and wealth, using religion as a pretext. If the people have no right of redress, those in charge can commit terrible atrocities. This is a structural issue.

Of course, certain domineering religious leaders have abused their role while others have been a benefit to society, as is true for any large organization, whether it be a government or large company. That doesn't mean that religion is at fault. Rather, religion has been misused to justify concepts like the divine right of kings, the religious persecution of other religions, and my (un)favorite: the burning of the Library of Alexandria, which destroyed much of the history of prehistoric times.

These abuses do not diminish the need for decent morality, which is the heart and soul of a humane religion.

I also think of all the good that has been done by religious organizations, from Catholic schools to hospitals and charitable works, including food banks, to praying for peace and encouraging good behavior, tolerance, and family life. The list could go on and on.

I do believe we would lose something precious if we were to lose religion altogether.

Writer John Longhurst asks the question, "Who will get involved with relief for natural disasters, run soup kitchens, co-ordinate aid for homeless people or deal with a hundred other kinds of social services when organized religion is gone?"[49]

There are a few beliefs which I hold in addition to the above ideas. You are born, you live, and you die. You cannot help where or to whom you are born. It can be to a millionaire's family or to a family in poverty.

---

[49] John Longhurst, "Some Denominations Built for a World that No Longer Exists." *Winnipeg Free Press*, September 10, 2022.

Either way, it will have an enormous impact on your early life. In some cases, you will have to rise above your beginnings. I did.

By the age of eighteen, it becomes your responsibility to face the rest of your life. Many people have become better educated and gone on to remarkable success. I don't respect those people who inherit great wealth and live idly and self-indulgently. But show me someone who lives a good life, works hard, is a productive citizen, is happily married, and has a family—and I respect that person.

I have always believed that death is inevitable. My paternal grandfather died when I was ten. My dad was heartbroken. I wrote a poem saying that my grandpa had lived a good life and would surely go to heaven, so why were we sad? We should celebrate his life and remember him with love.

I also believe in the KISS formula: keep it simple, stupid. If you try and identify the real problem, the solution often presents itself. Look for the nub of the issue, the bottleneck which impedes progress. Resolve it.

For example, Putin is trying to reinstate the prior Soviet system with all its shortcomings, including suppression and inefficiency. He is trying to blame the West for his lack of success, claiming that the West made him declare war on Ukraine. Russia is the worst-performing country of any major nation in "The Atlas of Impunity." That's his real problem.

Another example is the trickle-down theory in the U.S., which glorifies the rich, diminishes the poor, and has worked to eliminate the middle class, a process which Biden has stalled. But for how long?

I adhere to Christ's advice about how to tell truthful prophets from false ones. He said that we would be able to tell by the fruit of that person's seed. As an example, Donald Trump's presidency ended with the country being split in two. He was a Janus (the two-faced Roman god) to the people he appointed and then fired. He said that he could walk down a street and shoot someone and get away with it. He handled top secret documents affecting the security of the country in a cavalier fashion. Tell me he was a good prophet! Ha!

I created a creed for myself about thirty years ago during a period when Donna was having problems and I had an ugly incident at work that affected me deeply and made me think about my values. I only meant this creed for my own use, but I'll share it now.

VALUES
I am proud of my heritage,
and respect all people as equals;
I will promote faith, justice, and democracy;
I will cherish the earth;
I strive for simplicity, competence, and wisdom,
patience, compassion, and courage;
I shall maintain my composure in times of trouble,
and be humble in my successes;
I shall nourish my spirit, mind, and body;
Love my family and friends,
and live in fellowship with all.

CONCLUSION

I hope by now you can see why I referred to the "big picture" in Chapter One. I've commented on numerous topics and made observations and recommendations on many of them. So what are my concluding thoughts on all these issues? I have several.

The first is that we need to rejuvenate our religious institutions so they can provide the moral guidance our planet so desperately needs. In the final analysis, intellect alone does not inspire people. I hope I have provided enough information to inspire the clergy to renew their role in society, emphasizing the development of our individual souls and encouraging a reasonable set of guidelines for the public at large, as well as behaviors which are beneficial to preserving our home, Gaia. I hope that by doing so we bring about change in our fundamental belief systems so we can evolve and save ourselves and our planet.[50]

My second conclusion is that we must make clear to the leaders of the world, including the super-rich cabal of billionaires, that we must preserve our planet if our species is to have a future. If Gaia dies, so will they. No amount of money from exploiting nonrenewal resources is worth the destruction of our planet.

---

[50] If you believe that God is the supreme architect who created the universe and our world, then urging a congregation to act in ways which will protect his creation makes moral sense. Apparently, scientists are determining that the creation of a stable planet in a habitable zone around a sun is an extremely rare event.

A new theory has been advanced that we are the only living planet in the universe because earlier living planets had beings like us who destroyed their world by following the same path we are on.

There is a danger that human beings will be marginalized by people in power and replaced with artificial intelligence, robots, and genetic engineering available only to the elite. If this adversely affects the mass of humanity, think about what happened in Russia in 1917, not to mention the plot of *The Terminator*. In my view, the entire human race needs to be part of the system, with good governance for all. A.I. software needs to include a moral code, just as we humans do, to do no harm to humans, or in fact to all life.

Thirdly, I hope that I have given you a reason to appreciate and protect your own soul. That would be wonderful!

If I were to associate one word with this book, it would be *save*. Save morality! Save your soul! Save democracy! Save Gaia!

When I realized that a specific part of the brain is included in what I think of as the soul, my first thought was that this would somehow diminish the soul, making it something explainable, mechanical, and therefore kind of ordinary. But upon reflection, I realized that this part of the brain is the same area that gave us the genius of Newton and Einstein, the music of Beethoven and the Beatles, the works of Shakespeare, the insights of Buddha and Moses, the service of Florence Nightingale, and the singing of Andrea Bocelli. To me, it's like a beautiful stereo system, the mechanical components of which produce the most beautiful music—energy you cannot see but which has the most divine nature.

The same is true of the output of the creative minds of the people I just mentioned.

Of course, there are those with deranged minds, like Hitler, whose so-called music is more like a dirge, or the screeching sound which may be the noise from Putin's soul.

I hope the rest of us can make beautiful music together.

On that note, I thank you for reading my book—and I bid you adieu!

Before I close, however, I would like to offer one final comment. I am quite aware that it would take a miracle for everything I've proposed in this book to happen. So that is my final wish—for my dream to come true.

For you. For my grandchildren.